Legacies of Love
A Heritage of Queer Bonding

Legacies of Love
A Heritage of Queer Bonding

Winston Wilde, MA, DHS

The Haworth Press
Taylor & Francis Group
New York and London

For more information on this book or to order, visit
http://www.haworthpress.com/store/product.asp?sku=5890

or call 1-800-HAWORTH (800-429-6784) in the United States and Canada
or (607) 722-5857 outside the United States and Canada

or contact orders@HaworthPress.com

Published by

The Haworth Press, Taylor & Francis Group, 270 Madison Avenue, New York, NY 10016.

PUBLISHER'S NOTE
The development, preparation, and publication of this work has been undertaken with great care. However, the Publisher, employees, editors, and agents of The Haworth Press are not responsible for any errors contained herein or for consequences that may ensue from use of materials or information contained in this work. The Haworth Press is committed to the dissemination of ideas and information according to the highest standards of intellectual freedom and the free exchange of ideas. Statements made and opinions expressed in this publication do not necessarily reflect the views of the Publisher, Directors, management, or staff of The Haworth Press, Taylor & Francis Group, or an endorsement by them.

Poem on page 90 from T. E. Lawrence, *Seven Pillars of Wisdom,* from dedication to S. A., copyright 1926, 1935 by Doubleday, a division of Random House, Inc. Reprinted by permission.

A complete list of copyright acknowledgments for all images can be found on page 183.

Library of Congress Cataloging-in-Publication Data

Wilde, Winston.
    Legacies of love : a heritage of queer bonding / Winston Wilde.
      p. cm.
    Includes bibliographical references.
    ISBN: 978-1-56023-664-1 (hard : alk. paper)
    ISBN: 978-1-56023-665-8 (soft : alk. paper)
    1. Gay couples—History. 2. Love—History. 3. Gay men—Case studies. 4. Lesbians—Case studies. I. Title.

HQ76.25.W552 2007
306.76'6091821—dc22

                    2007011577

For John,
for giving me Happiness

For Paul,
for giving me Love

For Buddy,
for giving me life after deaths

And to the memory of Vern Bullough

NO LABOR-SAVING MACHINE

No labor-saving machine,
Nor discovery have I made,
Nor will I be able to leave behind me any wealthy bequest
    to found a hospital or library,
Nor reminiscence of any deed of courage for America,
Nor literary success nor intellect, nor book for the bookshelf,
But a few carols vibrating through the air I leave,
For comrades and lovers.

Walt Whitman, 1881

ABOUT THE AUTHOR

Winston Wilde, MA, DHS, is a sexologist and a psychotherapist in private practice in Beverly Hills. He is an adjunct professor at Antioch University, Los Angeles, teaching human sexuality and gender studies. His research includes pioneering studies into the sexualities of blind persons. Dr. Wilde has spoken internationally on the subject of queer love.

CONTENTS

Chapter 6. Pattern of Utopian Love   101

Chapter 7. Pattern of Peer Love   115

Foreword

In December 1973 the American Psychiatric Association took the controversial step of deleting homosexuality from the Association's compendium of psychiatric disorders. That action and the growing refusal of gay men and lesbians to remain invisible launched a movement to end discrimination against homosexuals that continues to reverberate in secular and religious debate.

In December 2006 New Jersey's legislature, ordered by its highest court to offer marriage or its equivalent to gay couples, voted to recognize civil unions for same-sex couples. In the words of the bill's chief sponsor, "Love counts. The gender of whom one loves should not matter to the state."

In these days of ideological warfare around same-gender marriage, this book articulates the growing consciousness that "love counts" regardless of "the gender of whom one loves."

Matter it has and matter it does. While queer bonding has been a reality of life for millennia, there are huge areas of this country and others where this love "dare not speak its name."

The beautiful stories of love that Winston Wilde has amassed in words and pictures break the ubiquitous culture of silence and invisibility that has shrouded queer bonding. Grounded in years of research, this scholarly work exposes the truth and integrity of same-gender love for all to see. In this respect it is a transgressive work as well as a healing antidote for cultures too long fettered by the taboo on queer bonding.

Before gay liberation there were women and men who consciously took a stand to be expressions of the love that dare not speak its name. In a world riddled with heterosexism and intolerance, these narratives of same-gender love flesh out the story of who we are as human beings.

In the words of the author, this "may not be a book that everyone in the family wants to read. But there is probably one person in every

Legacies of Love: A Heritage of Queer Bonding
© 2008 by The Haworth Press, Taylor & Francis Group. All rights reserved.
doi:10.1300/5890_a

family who could profit enormously from attaining this valuable information: that gay people *can* form meaningful relationships, and
they have for millennia."

Bishop Otis Charles

Acknowledgments

This book has been fourteen years in the making. There have been several hundred people along the way who have contributed in some way or another, far too many to mention. Please know that I honor your participation and support.

I extend my expressions of gratitude to the birthplace of this book, Antioch University, Los Angeles, and to all of my fabulous colleagues there, especially Eloise Klein Healy, who midwifed the conception of this book, David Tripp, Andrea Richards, Koreema Walden, and to the old-school folk, especially Benjamin Perkins, Keith Rand, and Christine Milrod.

To all of my old comrades in San Francisco: the Florettes, the Pervs and Sex-Positives, and especially to the Institute and Ted McIlvenna, an admitted heterosexual who supported me on this quest, I send my faithful thanks and praise. To all of my families in San Francisco, the living, the dead, and the in-between: the late Harvey, Otis and Felipe, Fakir and Carla, Ganymede, Neon, Sascha Bittner, Alex Mexi, Dana Peter Porras and his lover the late Marc Yim, Eileen and Auntie Ann, the late Cynthia Slater, the late teen angel, the late Greyson Slaughter, the late Marvin Feldman, and all of my thousands of late tribespeople. Oh, my Emerald City, I adore You.

Nods of great gratitude deservedly go to the following institutions for allowing me to pillage through their archives:

Academy of Motion Pictures Arts and Sciences Library, Beverly Hills
Antioch University, Los Angeles
Center for Sex Research, CSUN, Los Angeles
Institute for the Advanced Study of Human Sexuality, San Francisco
International Gay and Lesbian Archives, Los Angeles
June Mazer Lesbian Collection, West Hollywood

Legacies of Love: A Heritage of Queer Bonding
© 2008 by The Haworth Press, Taylor & Francis Group. All rights reserved.
doi:10.1300/5890_b

Lesbian Herstory Archives, Brooklyn, NY
Los Angeles Public Library, Downtown
New York Public Library, at 42nd Street
One Institute & Archives, USC, Los Angeles
Schomberg Center for Research in Black Culture, Harlem
Sexuality Information & Education Council
    of the United States, New York
UCLA Biomedical Library, Los Angeles
UCLA Special Collections Library, Los Angeles

Big heartfelt props, kudos, and appreciation go to Julie Cancio and Eric Harper for their valiant efforts in bringing this book to life. Julie and Eric undertook the Herculean chore of acquiring permissions to reprint photos and text, and it's the photos that give this book its vibrancy, literally putting faces to the stories. Muchas gracias.

A fraternal and adhesive thanks to the MoHos and all of my psychotherapy and sexology comrades, we soul warriors sounding the battle cry in our quixotic trenches, especially Jack Morin, Guy Baldwin, Eli Coleman, James Elias, Susan Hyatt, Joseph Kramer, the late Brian Miller, Marilyn Lawrence, Mary Nalick, Jose "Chapy" Orlando Hernandez Garcia (de Cuba), Kathy Sisson, Tristan Taormino (who activates my chi), Beverly Whipple, and certainly to Eve Kehr, my dancing analytic supervisor who is a delightfully hard enough object.

And to all of the men and women and others who have shared with me the stories of their experiences of love in their lives: my parents, their parents; my patients, who mean so much to me; my students, who teach me so much; my chela, whom I adore; my friends and families and tribespeople; my inherited mothers; neighbors and co-workers with whom I share my daily life. Thanks to all the perverts and outsiders who have opened their hearts to me, showing me new perspectives, and oddly, to all the strangers on public transportation who have confided their deepest sexual secrets to me. And ultimately, to those whose love I treasure: Douglas and Tita Caldwell, Lelia Moskowitz, Hari Grebler, Willow Evans, Don Shewey, The Puts, the late Don Allen, Tom Hyland, Judith and Richard, Greg and Lailani, Gay and Malka, Auntie Joy, Fernando Mejia, Ben Britt, Lisa Wolf, Darrel Couturier, Jack Daley, Michael Hill, Denny Kagasoff, Lisa Lyon, Elisabeth Nonas, Jordy, Tia, colten, and Magnus.

Thanks to the late Vern Bullough, a self-avowed heterosexual, for making the connection and providing the kiva, and to all the folks at The Haworth Press for making it happen.

Finally, to the people of whom this book speaks, for their courage to live lives that follow their hearts, and for embodying legacies of love.

Introduction

Back in 1968, I remember watching the television show *Hawaii Five-0* with my family in Santa Monica. In this cops-and-robbers TV show, the gay guys were always portrayed as loners, child molesters, humiliated perverts, and slimy criminals. I remember being angry about that because I knew it wasn't true. But what could I say? What could I do? I had my own little secrets to protect. I wanted to take a shower with my buffed-out gym coach. I wanted to sit naked with my best friend's dad. I was just as angry at myself.

My mom was a grad student at UCLA back then, and after school we would share our stories about what we each learned that day. I remember one day she came home from a psychology class and told me that homosexuals are sick, crazy, because it says so in the official psych book (*Diagnostic and Statistical Manual of Mental Disorders*, or DSM). I knew I wasn't sick or crazy, so it couldn't be true. That book must be wrong. But I hadn't yet empowered myself to speak up and give voice to the spirit of being queer.

My groovy mom continued her 1968 psychology lesson by saying that when homosexuals get older, no one will have sex with them, so they resort to prostitution. Eventually their money runs out and they become alcoholics. Most homosexuals commit suicide. She seemed to end the story there, with a really sad look on her face. *Jeez,* I thought, *this is worse than* Hawaii Five-O. I knew back then that I was a homo, but that none of those bad things was going to be my future.

But the part that hurt me the most was when she recounted her professor's lecture: homosexuals can't love. They are unable to form meaningful intimate relationships. All homosexuals are promiscuous and perverted, and their relationships never last. They are stuck and stunted in a psycho sickness that indicates that they will never have a

Legacies of Love: A Heritage of Queer Bonding
© 2008 by The Haworth Press, Taylor & Francis Group. All rights reserved.
doi:10.1300/5890_01

meaningful love partner. Holy moley, I knew this wasn't true either. I knew that someday I would find a man to love, a man who would love me back. I knew then that if I was going to find a way to have a life somewhere outside of *Hawaii Five-0* hell, the lobotomy chambers of the DSM, the electric chairs of state prisons, the local religious hate-spewers and the hallway bullies—well, I knew I had to find a way out, and that I'd better get busy.

I remember being a precocious and opinionated flower child. In my long hair and bellbottoms at age twelve, I was ravenous for knowledge about sex words. I would look them up in my 1968 *American Heritage Dictionary*: adultery, breast, clitoris, coitus, cunt, dyke, faggot, fairy, foreskin, gay, heterosexual, homosexual, lesbian, nipple, orgasm, penis, pervert, pussy, queer, sapphic, scrotum, semen, sex, sexuality, sperm, testicle, tribadism, vagina, vulva. I looked up: nude, naked, masturbate, fornicate, fuck, sodomy, sodomite, lewd, lascivious, licentious, prostitution, pedophilia, bestiality, and hermaphrodite. I knew I wasn't normal. My life as a sex researcher had begun.

What I was to learn later in life was that the definitions of words change over time, and that sexuality word definitions change even more rapidly. The word *homosexual* was invented in 1869, but not popularized for decades. Instead, the clinical term used through the latter half of the nineteenth century was *invert*: "inverts" suffer from "inversion." At that time the popular street term used for queer men was *bugger*. In the twentieth century, the word *gay* was used for decades by gay people before the popular culture adopted its usage.

When I was a teenager, the *Los Angeles Times* would always use the clinical word *homosexual* to define gay people, never using the friendlier term *gay*. They often employed adjective enhancers like *a self-avowed homosexual, an admitted homosexual, a confessed homosexual*. They would never use the word *gay* until the headlines read, "Gay Riots in SF."

Sometimes I prefer popular words over clinical words: I'd rather be a *bugger* than an *invert*, but, hey, that's just my preference. The word *gay* so much more defines who I am than does the word *homosexual*. Yet I really prefer the word *queer*, because it's edgy, artistic, outside of the mainstream of mediocrity. Queer is powerful. Queer captures my attention. I get to pucker my lips when I say it. Queer has a kiss in it. Queer is anarchic, and against the grain. Queer is unexpected, a pretty surprise, and lots of laughter amidst the ruins and the pain. Queer is tough and witty and odd. Queer is my spirituality and the manner in which I organize love.

What is love? Most poems are about love, as are most popular songs. Most great stories in history have a strong theme of love deeply embedded. Yet when I ask people what love means to them, it's amazing how varied and disparate their answers are. The ancient Greeks had about five different words to describe love, the ancient Persians had dozens of words, and in Hindi there are almost a hundred separate words to describe loves. But in English, as in most romantic languages, we have only one word to describe such a complex and intrinsic aspect of human experience. I am sorry to say, we Westerners are bankrupt in our ability to discuss love in any depth.

The *American Heritage Dictionary* (1968) will define love as: *a strong affectional attachment.* Those of you with knowledge of psychology will appreciate this subject/object definition. Those of you with training in Buddhism will remember that attachment brings suffering. Quantum physics teaches us that nothing remains static, that everything is made up of energy and molecules that are constantly in a state of rearranging. Therefore, to experience the attachment of love will inevitably create tragedy. The greatest love stories are tragedies. My late lover Paul warned me when we met: "The greater you love, the harder you fall."

Although love may create tragedy, it can also bring grand episodes of bliss and belonging: a ground of being. For some of us who are seekers, and who marshal the courage to venture, a loving relationship can be the ultimate path. Sometimes only through the mirror of our loving other half can we clearly see our features that stand to be improved. Opening one's self to a love relationship can be the most nourishing experience to be had in this great experiment of life.

Long-lasting love does not hold a more special place for me than short-lasting love. Sometimes couples stay together in unhappy love for far too long (such as **Barney** and **Brooks**), whereas other short-term loves (such as **Verlaine** and **Rimbaud**) are of great profundity. Once asked of a long-term older lesbian couple the key to their success, one of them answered, "A complete lack of creativity."

I have written hundreds of pages about love, and have shelves of books on the subject, from Plato to Tennov, from Ovid to Stendhal. To squish all that knowledge into a few paragraphs is utterly impossible. I can tell you that I know more about the history and philosophy of love than anyone I've met, and yet I feel at times as if I know almost nothing. I do know that loves are very much socially constructed, meaning that the social environment in which one lives will often dictate to some degree how the individual thinks about love, and thereby limit the person's concepts. For example, many people are in arranged marriages, and actually most humans on the planet are in such relationships, yet I hardly know anyone as such. Most of them do not at all conform to our Western ideas of love, specifically erotic love. It is estimated that half the people on the planet are polygamous (a man has more than one wife). Some cultures practice group or tribal marriage, fraternal marriage (men of a clan have a ceremony), or polyandry (a woman marrying more than one husband). The Islamic world has something called *sigeh,* or temporary marriage. People tend to think that everyone else is somewhat like they are. But they're not.

So I ask you to approach this book with an open mind, with the knowledge that the relationships discussed may not fit into previously conceived notions of what a love relationship should look like. In addition to the marriage styles just mentioned, people engage in many diverse love styles: pragma, storge, ludus, thea mania. Some people are polyamorous, which means that they love more than one person at a time.

The great psychiatrist Theodor Reik wrote that people don't fall in love, they jump. I like that distinction on many levels, specifically that it differentiates being a victim from being a courageous engager. I invite you to think of yourself as jumping into this book.

Where are all the queer love stories? Every time I lecture in public on this topic there are gay people in the audience who get angry. They stand, with tears in their eyes and open hands raised, asking, "Why didn't anyone tell me about this before? My life would have been so different."

History is the story of the victors; those who lose the war often lose the truth of who they are. In American History classes, are we ever taught that every treaty ever signed between a Native American tribe and the U.S. government was broken by the U.S. government? Were we ever taught that peanut butter was invented by a gay African

American (**George Washington Carver**)? No, we mostly only learn about the good deeds of straight white men.

In his speech to the Library of Congress in 1993, entitled *The Politics of Silence,* gay American writer **Paul Monette** said, "The will to silence the truth is everywhere as strong as the truth itself." He commented on famous acts perpetrated to silence queerdom: the burning of Aristotle's library at Alexandria, the Church's destruction of **Sappho**'s texts, the Nazi burning of **Magnus Hirschfeld**'s library, the 1993 censorship of a lesbian American writer. Queer history and queer truth are always in danger of being annihilated by the purveyors of dominant culture, because queer is, ipso facto, outside of the paradigm.

I remember in the first decade of the AIDS epidemic, as newspapers across this country published the obituaries of tens of thousands of gay American citizens, most periodicals refused to mention the deceased's "longtime companion." Gay love stories are often censored and denied.

In rereading my notes in preparation for writing this introduction, I came across a mission statement I wrote at the Four Seasons Hotel in New York in the early 1990s:

> My motivation for putting together *[Legacies of Love]* is simple. I just read the unbound galleys to *Straight from the Heart: A Love Story,* by Bob and Rod Jackson-Paris, and spoke to them on the phone. They told me how difficult it is for them to get the gay community to acknowledge the importance of their relationship. A couple of nights ago we had dinner with [Congressman] Barney Frank and Herb Moses who told me that neither the straight press nor the gay press will print a picture of the two of them. That he [Herb] is the first male in U.S. history to receive a congressional wife's pin, and that he and Barney dance together at the White House, but the photos in the paper the next day are always Barney dancing with a female. Then I realized that Paul [Monette] and I have been together for exactly three years now, and not once has the gay or straight press printed a photograph of the two of us. The current issue of *The Advocate* has only one photograph of two men touching: an advertisement for RSVP Cruises. The more I open my awareness to this issue, the more I see how gay and lesbian media perpetuate the straight stereotypes that queers are unable to bond. *The Advocate* ran a

cover story on [comedian] Kate Clinton: no photo of her with [her longtime lover] Urvashi [Vaid]. I want to create this book as a gift to queer people, of all ages and identities, to show that no matter what lies we were taught, gay and lesbian people have always loved, and we always will.

This project began for me as a personal quest to uncover stories of queer love. I needed to prove that what my mom learned in her psychology class at UCLA was wrong. Having well read my gay history, and knowing that many illustrious persons in history were homosexual, I wondered, Who were their lovers? We know about **Leonardo da Vinci,** but who were his lovers? Who was **Eleanor Roosevelt**'s lover? Who were the lovers of writers **Tennessee Williams, Mary Renault, André Gide, Willa Cather, Edward Carpenter, Radclyffe Hall, W. H. Auden**? Or anthropologist **Ruth Benedict**? What kinds of relationships did they have? I'd heard of Gertrude and Alice, but then discovered in research another lesbian couple, just as fabulous, with the same first names: **Gertrude Tate** and **Alice Austen**. Who were the lovers of movie stars **Rudolph Valentino, Cary Grant, Greta Garbo, Rock Hudson**? Who shared lives with the great musical composers **Stephen Foster, Benjamin Britten, Freddie Mercury,** or with the great painters **Rosa Bonheur** and **Romaine Brooks**?

Of the several methods employed to gather data for this project, my favorite was visiting the dead. As archaeologists search for the stelae—-the gravestones inscribed and adorned—-Paul taught me to search out cemeteries whenever traveling to make pilgrimage to our ancestors. One of the grooviest graveyards in the world is the Protestant Cemetery in Rome, where one finds glorious fruits of the earth. When Paul and I were there with our friends Gay and Malka, Gay took a photo of Paul leaning on John Keats's grave, while I'm leaning on Joseph Severn's. Across the way are the twin graves of Percy Bysshe Shelley and Edward J. Trelawny. Shelley was a poet who lived an extraordinary life, and died young in a freak boating accident; his young lover Trelawny survived. On Shelley's gravestone is inscribed:

> Nothing of him that doth fade,
> But doth suffer a sea-change
> Into something rich and strange

And next to Shelley, a matching gravestone placed decades later, says of Edward J. Trelawny:

THESE ARE TWO FRIENDS WHOSE LIVES WERE UNDIVIDED
SO LET THEIR MEMORY BE NOW THEY HAVE GLIDED
UNDER THE GRAVE LET NOT THEIR BONES BE PARTED,
FOR THEIR TWO HEARTS IN LIFE WERE SINGLE HEARTED.

Well, you can't get much more queer than that.

There are numerous limitations to this project. I would not at all consider it scientific. I randomly selected legendary people, mostly homosexual, whom I have admired or entertained a curiosity about. This in itself is obviously a great bias.

My goal has been to be more inclusive than exclusive in selecting legends. From the beginning I made a determined effort to make sure that women's stories were included in this book, and more than half of the people represented here were biologically female.

To me, some bisexuals are more queer than some homosexuals, and so I've included some bisexuals: **Margaret Mead, Hilda Doolittle, Colette.** To me, some heterosexuals are queerer than some homosexuals, and so I've included some: **Havelock Ellis, Kenneth Mac-**

pherson, Lucien Happersberger. And to me, many transgendered people are queer, no matter what their sexualities may be, so in this book I've included some: **Queen Christina of Sweden, Calamity Jane, Wagetote.**

There will be naysayers and doubters and historians with credentials who will pick these stories apart in attempts to discredit it all. America's a free country, and the world's a big place, so they can say whatever they want. People say that queers are sick and sinful, and there's even a president who wants to amend the Constitution of the United States of America to say that same-gender relationships are not as valuable as opposite-gender relationships, and therefore queer love should be codified as second class.

I am a passionate queer romantic and I cherish these legends of my ancestors. But be warned: they are not all pretty. Does not every tribe have some legacy of shame? I am against omitting the truth, and so have included in this collection: American bullies **J. Edgar Hoover** and **Clyde Tolson,** murderers **Nathan Leopold** and **Richard Loeb,** and raging alcoholics **Paul Verlaine** and **Arthur Rimbaud.** Some of these legendary folk were misogynist, racist, even homophobic.

Most of these stories are of queer American love legends, with entire countries and regions not yet represented herein. There are a lot more stories of white people than of people of color. There are a lot of writers, because they create evidence of themselves and because I'm attracted to them. If I were more interested in sports, there would probably be more athletes represented. I would like to preface this book with an apology to anyone who feels that their tribe is not adequately represented, and an invitation to all readers in the world to contact me with more evidence of diverse legendary lovers to be included in a future edition.

Most of the research on these lovers was done pre-Internet, fresh into my second widowhood. I cannot accurately describe for you the fresh grief I experienced over and over each time I discovered another fabulous constellation of queer lovers, only to have to, at some point, stop researching them and move on to the next couple. The multiple losses of love were agony. But, I think it was Auden who once said that one never finishes a book; one simply decides when to abandon it.

While collecting these love stories I noticed certain patterns emerging. These seven patterns of legendary love, which comprise the text of this book, are not meant to be finite nor all-inclusive. A significant gay male pattern not mentioned here is the ludic lover, the man who loves everyone he is with, with no commitment to anyone, sometimes referred to as a *sacred intimate*. **Walt Whitman**'s love poem to New York, "City of Orgies," is perhaps the national anthem of ludic love.

This book is organized by patterns of love. The patterns are presented in no particular order of importance: heterogender, intergenerational, overlapping, interclass, interethnic, utopian, and peer. Each chapter begins with a brief description or definition of that particular pattern, followed by the legacies of that pattern. Please note that many legacies fall under more than one pattern, i.e., **Lawrence of Arabia** and **Ahmed Dahoum** were both interethnic lovers and intergenerational lovers.

The legacies as expressed here may appear a bit encyclopedic. This is intentional. I am giving you the facts as I have found them, with great efforts to not embellish the stories whatsoever. Obviously, historians disagree with one another as to the absolute truths: friends fight over misunderstandings; adult siblings recall their childhoods quite differently; some people fabricate stories in their letters and journals; queer realities are often shamefully omitted from documentation; families destroy evidence of their relatives' homosexuality. I know from working as a therapist with couples, and from observing humanity, that in relationships two people often view the relationship from different perspectives and remember different aspects. And then our perceptions of the past are altered by new lived experiences. Here and there in the book I will say that I am speculating about this or that, but generally speaking I leave it to the archives to speak for themselves.

Following the patterns, you will find a glossary to help in understanding some of the terminology used in this book. Most of these words are about love, sex, and mating.

I cannot present the stories of these lovers in entirety; in fact, I make no attempt to do so. So many of these lovers lived big, grand lives. Some of these legends have a half-dozen books written about them, with authors squabbling about the truths of their stories. Many sources of reference are in conflict about dates of birth, who cheated on who first, etc. The Internet has facilitated the dissemination of both information and misinformation. I've done my best to provide the most accurate data, but have no doubt that there will be an occasional inadvertent misrepresentation.

Some of these legends have no books or journals or letters to tell us much at all. We have only fragments of evidence from which to preserve these precious loves. They are stories preserved from the conspiracy of silence, the loves that dare not speak their names.

As well, I could not possibly mention every queer lover who ever lived. Nor have I included the great queer myths of the planet, perhaps the oldest love story of humankind, Gilgamesh and Enkidu (Mesopotamia); and let's not forget Ruth and Naomi, David and Jonathan, Set and Horus (Egyptian), Achilles and Patroclus, Zeus and Ganymede, Xu Jifang and Yu Ruilang, Sedna and Qailertetang, White Shell Woman, Turquoise Boy, Batman and Robin, Tonto and the Lone Ranger, to name a few.

The carols of comrades I bring to you in this book are stories of true love. This is an ongoing project that I invite you to help grow.

If, as the anthropologists say, the television has replaced the campfire as the focal point for cultural storytelling, then America has come a long way in forty years. No longer in America do we see the blatant *Hawaii Five-0* hatred of gay people in our network primetime stories. In fact, most of our televised cultural stories now have a gay or lesbian character included. But do we see them yet kiss, or be sexual, or even love? Are they ever meaningfully partnered? I would argue that the true spirit of queer love is bigger than television and bigger than America. These love stories are everywhere on the planet, waiting to be remembered.

Chapter 1

Pattern of Heterogender Love

We are sure of each other, in this odd, strange, detached, intimate, mystical relationship which we could never explain to any outside person.

Vita Sackville-West to Harold Nicolson
(Nicolson, 1973, p. 188)

Heterogender love is a coupling of at least one male with at least one female. Their relationship may or may not be sexual. Some heterogender lovers marry as openly gay or lesbian individuals, such as in the case of **Jane and Paul Bowles,** while others come out to themselves and others after they are married, such as **Harold Nicolson** and **Vita Sackville-West.** Heterogender love is also found in bisexuals **(H.D., Margaret Mead, Will Geer)** and in transgendered people (**Calamity Jane,** George Sand).

Heterogender love is a way to survive a homophobic society. In places where homosexuals have been actively persecuted, such as the military, Hollywood, educational institutions, and the government, lesbians and gay men have often paired up to avoid detection and discrimination. This love style is usually a domestic arrangement of companionate love, wherein family approval, financial status (sometimes an inheritance), and job security are obtained. However pragmatic this style may appear, sometimes, with Aphrodite's blessings, an unexpected great affectionate love bond is shared.

Legacies of Love: A Heritage of Queer Bonding
© 2008 by The Haworth Press, Taylor & Francis Group. All rights reserved.
doi:10.1300/5890_02

JANE BOWLES AND PAUL BOWLES

Jane Sydney (née Auer) Bowles (February 22, 1917-May 4, 1973), American writer. Jane is reported to have often entered rooms and proclaimed, "I'm Jewish and I'm a lesbian." Her body of work is small, her most noted work being the novel *Two Serious Ladies* (1943). She suffered from a limp due to a childhood operation, and from many illnesses: alcoholism, substance abuse, manic depression, breakdowns, suicide attempts, and a serious stroke at age forty, which left her disabled.

Jane and Paul Bowles, Tangier, 1949

Paul Frederic Bowles (December 30, 1910-November 18, 1999), American writer, composer. After **Gertrude Stein** told Paul to give up being a poet, he studied music and collaborated with his friends Aaron Copland and Leonard Bernstein. Paul later began writing again, notably *The Sheltering Sky* (1949).

Paul and Jane met at a pot party in Harlem (1937) and married a year later. Jane was self-identified as a lesbian who had had several lesbian relationships and a few affairs. She is remembered as being seductive and sexually capricious. Paul self-identified as bisexual but is most known for his affairs with young Arab men, notably Moroccan painter Ahmed Yacoubi and later Mohammed Mrabet. It is alleged as part of the great mystique of Jane's sexuality that she had a couple of affairs with men, but she assured a friend that she would never engage in heterosexual activity, as it would deeply upset her husband.

This heterogendered queer couple settled in Tangier, Morocco (1948), where they hosted many queer writers (Truman Capote, **Tennessee Williams, Jack Kerouac,** Allen Ginsburg, Wiiliam S. Burroughs, **Christopher Isherwood,** Susan Sontag) and countless illustrious persons (notably rock star Mick Jagger).

Jane Bowles converted to Catholicism (c.1971) and died in a convent hospital in Málaga, Spain, where she is buried in an unmarked grave at San Miguel Cemetery. Paul Bowles' ashes are interred in Lakemont, New York.

BIBLIOGRAPHY

Dillon, Millicent (1981). *A Little Original Sin: The Life and Work of Jane Bowles.* New York: Anchor Books, Doubleday.

CALAMITY JANE AND WILD BILL HICKOK

Martha Jane Cannary (c. May 1, 1852-August 1, 1903), American frontier character, sex worker. We don't rightly know a whole lot about Calamity Jane; she was a fibber and boastful and often drunk. Calamity Jane was a legend in her own time, a performance artist and cross-dressing pistol-packing, cigar-smoking frontier woman. Jane's childhood out West was tragic. She was an orphan, and from studies we have today, one could speculate that she was sexually abused as a child (one indicator being her early entry into prostitution). The Wyoming *Cheyenne Sun* described Jane at sixteen as "a young stray with the spirit of original sin." At times I think of Calamity Jane as a gay man trapped in a woman's body.

Calamity Jane and Wild Bill Hickok

Calamity Jane was notorious throughout the West for her lifetime career as a sex worker, and for shooting up saloons that refused service to women. By all accounts (except Hollywood's) Calamity Jane is described as masculine, butch, gruff, explosive, aggressive, and acting in unladylike ways, such as smoking, drinking, cursing, being sexual, wearing pants, not riding sidesaddle, and carrying guns and using them well. Despite her gender nonconformity in dress and manner, Jane appears to have been entirely heterosexual. She evidently practiced serial marriage; she claimed eleven husbands, but written documentation suggests only two. The latter marriage (1885) was to Clinton "Charley" Burk, whose surname she retains on her tombstone. The daughter they gave up for adoption proved to be his from a previous marriage.

Her other documented marriage (1871) was to James Butler Hickok (May 27, 1837-August 2, 1876), American frontier character, marshal, gunfighter. Wild Bill Hickok, a fastidious, well-groomed dandy, was notorious for his obsession with fine clothing—he always wore a Prince Albert—and for his fondness of cologne. He started as a stagecoach driver who gained fame as a gunfighter. Wild Bill served the federal government as a scout for the Union Army during the Civil War, and as deputy U.S. marshal at Fort Riley (1866), and marshal of Hays, Kansas (1869), and Abilene, Texas (1871). If you were looking for Wild Bill, townsfolk would probably point you over to the Chinamen's house, because Wild Bill had a soft spot for smoking opium. He met Calamity Jane in 1870. But their union did not last long, and in 1873 Calamity Jane gave up her daughter for adoption, Wild Bill denying that the child was his.

Wild Bill had an intimate fifteen-year relationship hitched up with Colorado Charley (née Charles H. Utter, 1838-unknown), American entrepreneur. Like Wild Bill, Colorado Charley was known as a dandy who always wore a white vest and lots of "gaudy jewelry." Legends of Wild Bill and Colorado Charley are testament to the manly attachments of pards on the frontier. Colorado Charley insisted on bathing daily, even when prospecting in winter. He disappeared while on an expedition.

Both men had previously married women: Wild Bill married (1876) Madame Agnes Lake Thatcher, an affluent equestrienne, but left her in less than three weeks. Colorado Charley, at twenty-eight, married (1866) Matilda Nash, fifteen, but left her in less than two

Arapahoe Joe, Wild Bill Hickok, Buffalo Bill Cody and his pard Texas Jack Omoohundro, and Colorado Charley

weeks. I would speculate that something wasn't happening in those marriages.

Poor Calamity Jane, widowed, destitute and alcoholic, turned to her friend Buffalo Bill for employment (1893) in his traveling Wild West Show. She died knowing that her outlandish legend was grander than her life. Calamity Jane and Wild Bill Hickok are buried together at Mount Moriah Cemetery in Deadwood, South Dakota. Colorado Charley was responsible for Wild Bill's interment, and on his headstone wrote:

> . . . Pard, we will meet again
> in the happy hunting ground,
> to part no more . . .

This briefly intense heterogendered love of Calamity Jane and Wild Bill was a short chapter in both of their illustrious lives. And yet they are buried side by side, preserving their heteroqueer legacy into eternity.

Their intergenerational relationship is better understood when removed from the limiting constructs of sexual orientation and gender identification, and instead observed as a case of heterogendered bonding of two queer people.

BIBLIOGRAPHY

Spring, Agnes Wright (1968). *Colorado Charley, Wild Bill's Pard.* Denver, CO: Pruett Press, Inc.

AMELIA EARHART AND GEORGE PALMER PUTNAM

Amelia Earhart (July 24, 1897-July 2, 1937), American aviator. Earhart was a tomboy from Kansas who moved around much of her life, changing direction at whim. She is most famous as a pioneering woman aviator who was lost at sea. Earhart broke at least twelve records for speed, distance, altitude, and solo flights. She was also the first woman to succeed in transatlantic flight, and the first human to achieve this twice. Earhart traveled the country lecturing and promoting feminism. She authored two books, *20 Hrs. 40 Min.* (1928) and *The Fun of It* (1932). Earhart was femme and butch; she was a homemaker and liked to shop for scarves, yet she also liked to get her hands dirty tinkering with airplane engines. She drove a gravel truck to help pay for her flight lessons. In a letter to her sister she described her first flight instructor (and possible lover) Neta Snook: "She dresses and talks like a man and can do everything around a plane a man can do. I'm lucky that she'll teach me" (Grier and Reid, 1976, p. 80).

Earhart with Putnam, prior to taking off for Puerto Rico from Miami, June 1937

Earhart wore brown to her wedding (1930) to George Palmer

Putnam (1887-1950), American publicist, explorer. Their intergenerational relationship was far from conventional. Shortly before their marriage, Earhart wrote to Putnam, "In our life together I shall not hold you to any medieval code of faithfulness to me, nor shall I consider myself bound to you similarly" (Grier and Reid, 1976, pp. 82-84). Biographers agree it was an arranged marriage of convenience. Archival interviews place Earhart as an intimate of her mother-in-law, visiting in New York (c. 1931) a "raunchy drag show" at Sammy's Bowery Follies, and a drag ball at Harlem's Savoy Ballroom. She was also reported to be escorted by lesbian friends to the oldest lesbian club in America, in Greenwich Village, the Sampsonetts!. Similarly, legend has it that Putnam, who was of the Putnam Publishing empire, was gay and openly frequented gay hangouts.

Substantial evidence does not exist (yet), in this reviewer's opinion, to conclude the sexual orientations of either Earhart or Putnam. Putnam was married before Earhart, and twice after. But then, **Cary Grant** was married five times. Putnam's first wife, Dorothy Binney, bore two sons from their union. Binney was a notorious Hollywood lesbian, a stuntwoman who threw all-girl parties attended by Earhart and lesbian-American actress Nancy "Miss Hathaway" Culp.

Earhart was most certainly a gender-variant woman who oftentimes preferred the company of strong, independent women, many of whom were lesbian. Sadly, many of the important details of this legendary couple's life together are perhaps forever lost at sea.

BIBLIOGRAPHY

"Earhart's Legacy Soars On." *Daily News,* Los Angeles, July 24, 1991.

Grier, Barbara and Reid, Coletta (eds.) (1976). *Lesbian Lives: Biographies of Women from* The Ladder. Oakland, CA: Diana Press.

Interview of Harry Otis, *In Touch,* #21.

Ware, Susan (1994). *Still Missing: Amelia Earhart and the Search for Modern Feminism.* New York: W.W. Norton and Co.

George Palmer Putnam and Amelia Earhart

RUDOLPH VALENTINO AND NATACHA RAMBOVA
AND ALLA NAZIMOVA

We may never know exactly what their relationship was, but their legends are inextricable. Rodolpho Alfonzo Raffaelo Pierre Filibert Guglielmi di Valentina D' Antonguolla (winner of the *Legacies of Love* Longest Name Award) (May 6, 1895-August 23, 1926), Italian-American silent film star, dancer. Rudy's family sent him away to America (1913) in hopes that he'd make money. He first lived in New York, spoke no English, and held a variety of very odd jobs. Rudy got into trouble with the police several times. He married (1919) lesbian-American actress Jean Acker who locked him out of the bridal suite on their wedding night, calling the marriage "a big mistake." Acker then moved in with "an intimate friend," Grace Darmond. Their divorce was granted on the grounds that their marriage was unconsummated.

Natacha Rambova and Rudolph Valentino

Rudolph Valentino starred in many silent films, notably *The Sheik* (1921), *Blood and Sand* (1922), and *The Son of the Sheik* (1926). Valentino was one of Hollywood's earliest male sex symbols and was often referred to as "the love god." It was reported that heterosexual women would faint in movie theaters, overcome by Rudy's erotic allure. Valentino augmented his earnings by dancing professionally, including a gig in San Francisco. He practiced fencing, was an accomplished equestrian, and inhabited his body with fortitude and grace.

Natacha Rambova (née Winifred Shaughnessy, January 19, 1897-June 3, 1966), American actor, set and costume designer. Natacha was born in Salt Lake City, Utah, but is reported to have told people that she was a Russian countess. She acted in many theatrical productions but was the lead in only one movie, aptly titled, *When Love Grows Cold* (1925).

Alla Nazimova (née Nasimoff, June 4, 1879-July 13, 1945), Russian-American stage and screen actress, artistic director. Born in Yalta, Crimea, Russia, to a wealthy Jewish family, Nazimova was sent away to a Catholic school in Switzerland. She studied music at

Alla Nazimova and Rudolph Valentino in *Camille*, 1921

the St. Petersburg Conservatory and was an accomplished violinist. But she gave up music for acting and studied under Stanislavsky in Moscow. There she married fellow Russian actor Paul Orleneff, with whom she traveled in a theater company and settled in New York (1905). Despite her pleas, he refused to grant her a divorce. Most of Nazimova's stage productions *(A Doll's House, Salome)* were of a feminist theme. She moved to Hollywood and starred in a dozen silent films and is noted for influencing future film stars

Gloria Swanson and **Greta Garbo.** Nazimova at her peak (1920s) was earning $13,000 a week. She was the owner of Mary's, a lesbian bar on the Sunset Strip, and developed the famed Garden of Allah Hotel on Sun- set and Crescent Heights Boulevards in West Hollywood. The Garden of Allah, with its three-plus lushly landscaped acres, bungalows, and swimming pool in the shape of the Black Sea, was a notorious magnet for gay and lesbian hotshots of Los Angeles in the 1930s. Nazimova was a well-liked and powerful Hollywood lesbian who had many affairs, notably with **Mercedes de Acosta** and Dolly Wilde (**Oscar Wilde**'s niece). Nazimova was Nancy Reagan's godmother.

Rambova and Nazimova were lovers (1920) while collaborating on the film *Camille* (1921). Nazimova was the producer and female lead, Rambova the set designer and art director. When the fledgling Italian actor Rudolph Valentino walked by the set one day, Nazimova said to Rambova that he was the perfect male lead to play opposite her. Rambova didn't like him, but she acquiesced. *Camille* was a big success that catapulted all three of their careers. Rambova is reported to have had an overbearing personality, to have been very pushy and not well-liked in Hollywood; she was later contractually banned from Valentino's sets. Natacha meddled in Rudy's life and dominated his every decision. Rambova thought that American women were responding to his sensitive nature and so she costumed him ever more effeminately. In *The Young Rajah* (1922), Rambova draped Valentino in almost nothing but pearls and full-face makeup, the envy, no doubt, of every drag queen in America. The *Chicago Tribune* printed a vitriolic lambasting of Valentino entitled, "Pink Powder Puffs," referring to "Rudy . . . that painted pansy" (Wallace et al., 1981, p. 514). Valentino's career was ruined by Rambova's bad advice. But he was loyal to her and they decided to marry, perhaps as a front of manly heterosexuality.

As a fluke, when Valentino and Rambova returned from their quickie wedding (1922) in Mexicali, Mexico, Valentino was arrested for bigamy. At the time, California law required one year to pass after divorce before remarrying. The headlines of Rudolph Valentino being accused of having more than one female in his harem led to hysteria among his female fans. His stellar celebrity was instantly reinstated. Valentino divorced Rambova (1925), and left her one dollar in his will.

Valentino was often seen in his last year with actress Pola Negri on his arm. Negri had earlier participated in a public relations stunt to make gay-American actor **William Haines** appear heterosexual. Tallulah Bankhead—a lady not known to mince words—referred to Negri as "a lying lesbo, a Polish publicity hound" (Hadleigh, 1994a, p. 215).

Valentino died suddenly at age thirty-one of a perforated ulcer. He was entombed at Hollywood Memorial Park Cemetery. Valentino had been deeply in debt, and his entire estate was auctioned off, including all personal effects. Even his personal diaries were auctioned off, with pages torn out. But one homoerotic entry (1924) escaped the censors. After describing picking up a guy at a gay bar on Wilshire Boulevard, Valentino wrote: "I went back with him to his home . . . I was wildly passionate . . .We made love like tigers until dawn."

Rambova had many women lovers in her years in Hollywood. She later married (1934) Spanish nobleman Don Alvaro de Urzaiz of Majorca, and left him soon thereafter.

Nazimova was a lesbian who lived with a male companion, actor/director Charles Bryant, whom she separated from in 1925. In the late 1920s, Nazimova left Hollywood to return to Broadway, but in the 1940s she returned to Hollywood for occasional cameos, notably *In Our Time* (1944) and *The Bridge of San Luis Rey* (1944). Her ashes are buried at Forest Lawn Memorial Park, Glendale, California.

Both Valentino and Nazimova have stars in their honor on Hollywood's legendary Walk of Fame.

BIBLIOGRAPHY

Hadleigh, Boze (1994a). *Hollywood Babble On: Stars Gossip About Other Stars.* New York: Barricade Books.

Hadleigh, Boze (1994b). *Hollywood Lesbians.* New York: Barricade Books.

Mackensie, Norman A. (1974). *The Magic of Rudolph Valentino.* London: The Research Publishing Company.

Scagnetti, Jack (1975). *The Intimate Life of Rudolph Valentino.* New York: Jonathan David Publishing.

Wallace, Irving, Wallace, Amy, Wallechinsky, David, and Wallace, Sylvia (eds.) (1981). *The Intimate Sex Lives of Famous People.* New York: Delacorte Press.

HAVELOCK ELLIS AND EDITH ELLIS

. . .a union of affectionate comradeship, in which the specific
emotions of sex had the small-
est part, yet a union, as I was
later to learn by experience,
able to attain even on that basis
a passionate intensity of love.

Havelock Ellis
on his relationship with Edith Ellis
(Grosskurth, 1985, p. 141)

Edith and Havelock Ellis, 1896

Henry Havelock Ellis (February 2,
1859-July 8, 1939), British sexologist, physician, writer. Havelock Ellis
was perhaps the most prominent
sexologist of his time. He wrote more
than fifty volumes, seven of which—
written over a forty-year period—comprise his most well-known
Studies in the Psychology of Sex. Ellis's *The Dance of Life* (1923)
deeply inspired gay-American dancer **Ted Shawn.**

Edith Mary Ellis (née Lees, March 9, 1861-September 13, 1916),
British writer and pamphleteer, lecturer, lesbian feminist. Edith was a
lesbian when she married Havelock on December 19, 1891. She
wrote in one of her many pamphlets (1892):

> The very root of the whole sex question is the absolute eco-
> nomic and social independence of woman, so that love may be
> freed from commercialism and able to clearly face its own
> needs. In order to attain this we shall inevitably have to try ex-
> periments which will bring social ostracism on those who have
> the honesty to put their principles into action. (Grosskurth,
> 1985, p. 145)

Smashing the shackles of Victorian conformity, more fascinated
by transcendental communities and alternative modes of living, Edith
and Havelock were truly pioneers of the queer family. Their heterogendered companionate marriage remained loving and faithful until

Edith's death. They retained sexual and financial independence; Havelock made money from writing articles for (mostly) medical journals, Edith had a small income from an inheritance. They split the cost of her wedding ring. They traveled throughout much of their marriage, often separately, never missing a day of letter-writing to each other.

Edith's strong femme nature fascinated Havelock: she didn't neatly fit into his sexological categorizations of lesbians. Encouraging a colleague to study lesbians, he wrote: "My wife . . . can supply cases of inversion [homosexuality] in women from among her own friends" (Grosskurth, 1985, p. 178). Most of Havelock and Edith's friends were gays and lesbians, most notably **Edward Carpenter** and John Addington Symonds. Havelock wrote the foreword to the first edition of *The Well of Loneliness* for their friend **Radclyffe Hall.** Women writers **H.D.** and **Bryher** credited Havelock's compassion and advice with saving their relationship. Havelock joined **Emma Goldman** in her global campaign against "outing." And he is possibly the first European recorded to have experimented with mescal buttons (1897). Ellis wrote of turning on his friends Arthur Symons (an avowed heterosexual), and William Butler Yeats and his lover Edward Martyn one night in a London hotel room.

Many people had reported Havelock as being almost asexual, an unexpected analysis of the man who wrote more about sexology than perhaps any other human being ever. Some biographers dubiously speculate that Havelock was "impotent," while others believe he was a urolophile (liked a little piss with his sex). Toward the end of his life he confided in a letter to his dearest friend, lesbian American reproductive rights advocate Margaret Sanger, that he suffered from what sexologists today refer to as rapid ejaculation.

Havelock had two other major romantic love interests: Olive Schreiner and Françoise Lafitte. Edith had a succession of passionate and tempestuous lesbian relationships. My feminist heart lusts for a biography of Edith Ellis.

BIBLIOGRAPHY

Grosskurth, Phyllis (1985). *Havelock Ellis.* New York: New York University Press.

VITA SACKVILLE-WEST AND HAROLD NICOLSON

Harold Nicolson and Vita Sackville-West with Rollo on the steps of the Tower, 1955

We are sure of each other, in this odd, strange, detached, intimate, mystical relationship which we could never explain to any outside person.

Vita to Harold
(Nicolson, 1973, p. 188)

I just look on you as the person whom I love best in the world, and without whom life would lose all its light and meaning.

Harold to Vita
(Nicholson, 1973, p. 168)

Victoria Mary Sackville-West (March 9, 1892-June 2, 1962), British aristocrat, novelist and poet. Vita wanted badly to inherit the castle she grew up in, Knole, which boasted seven courtyards (one for each day of the week), fifty-two staircases, and 365 rooms, but patriarchy defeated her and the estate went to a male cousin. Her fifty books include poetry, novels, short stories, biographies, and her later claim to fame, gardening books.

Harold George Nicolson (November 21, 1886-May 1, 1968), British writer, diplomat. Harold wrote more than forty books, one of which earned him his knighthood (1953), but his most notable contributions were political. Nicolson was elected to the House of Commons. He also served at the League of Nations and at the Paris Peace Conference.

Vita and Harold married on October 1, 1913, and remained lovingly faithful for half of a century. Their sexual relations discontinued after the birth of their second son, Nigel. Harold admitted to his wife that he was gay. Vita admitted that she'd had an affair with her childhood friend Rosamund Grosvenor, and that she indeed was perhaps a sapphic lover. Their companionate marriage was based on honesty and trust, surviving Harold's many incidental homosexual flings and Vita's two serious love affairs. It is reported that Harold never found romantic love with his sexual partners, but instead reserved this love for Vita.

Vita left her marriage and children (May 19, 1919) for a passionate three year "elopement" with Violet Keppel Trefusis. Harold wrote (February 3, 1919): "I feel you are slipping away, you who are my anchor, my hope and all my peace. Dearest, you don't know my devotion to you. What you do, can never be wrong. I love you, in a mad way, *because* of it all" (Nicolson, 1973, p. 156); and (November 1, 1919): "You are the best and most sacred and the most tender thing in my life" (p. 144). Vita returned to Harold and their family.

After eighteen years of not speaking, Violet fled war-torn France and telephoned Vita upon arriving in England. Vita wrote, "We loved each other too deeply for too many years, and we must not play with fire again."

Her third profound lesbian love was with Bloomsbury queen Virginia Woolf. Vita and Virginia had sexual interaction only twice, but their romantic friendship lasted for life. Woolf has been described as "sexually cold" and "frigid" (Nicolson, p. 206), and her sexless companionate marriage to heterosexual Leonard Woolf complemented that of Vita and Harold's bizarre arrangement. The four spent much time together.

Harold and Vita in Harold's study at Sissinghurst, 1932

The heterogendered coupling of lesbian Vita Sackville-West and homosexual Harold Nicolson is testament to a particular tradition of queer love. It didn't matter that Harold brought his tricks to breakfast with Vita and her *chérie du jour.* These legendary lovers never compromised their faithfulness to each other.

I know that your love for me is central, as is my love for you, and it's quite unaffected by what happens at the outer edge.

Harold to Vita
(Nicolson, 1973, p. 206)

BIBLIOGRAPHY

Nicolson, Nigel (1973). *Portrait of a Marriage.* New York: Atheneum.

Chapter 2

Pattern of Intergenerational Love

It is the happy heart that breaks.

Sara Teasdale
(Teasdale, 1937, p. 140)

Intergenerational love is a relationship of two (or more) same-gender persons with ten years or greater difference in age, or of a perceived significant age difference (for example, ages fifteen and twenty-three). Sometimes called *chronophilia,* intergenerational lovers may eroticize their age difference.

Studies indicate that one-third of gay and lesbian relationships are intergenerational. This love style is of profound traditional importance to queer love, from the ancient worlds to the present. In what can sometimes be perceived as a mentoring process, the younger partner is given access (social, political, financial), guidance (moral, spiritual, practical), role modeling, and education of traditional queer life and history. The senior partner is given vitality and invigoration, access to the new generation's perspectives and culture, opportunities to parent and of benefaction, and to sow seeds for a healthy and vibrant future queerdom. In a personal conversation with **Don Bachardy** about his thirty-year tempestuous relationship with **Christopher Isherwood**—thirty years his senior—I asked Don, "What made your relationship work?" He explained that it worked because they were of such different positions, there was no competition, a common stumbling block for many male-male relationships.

This collection of intergenerational lovers is really quite astounding. I present to you here legendary lovers who are considered to be the finest exemplars in their century of writers, inventors, dancers, anthropologists, athletes, thinkers, poets, priests, and prophets of love. Enjoy.

Legacies of Love: A Heritage of Queer Bonding
doi:10.1300/5890_03

SOCRATES AND ALCIBIADES

Socrates (c. 469-399 BCE), Athenian philosopher. Socrates had an ordinary childhood; his father was a sculptor, his mother a midwife. He was not well-educated but had a penchant for asking questions. This led to his *Socratic* method of teaching. It is reported that Socrates married "a shrew" named Xantippe and had three sons. The oracle at Delphi proclaimed Socrates as the smartest man alive (c. 429 BCE). Socrates disagreed with this prophecy and stated that he would prove God wrong.

As a soldier on the battlefield, Socrates rescued the life of his wounded young pupil and lover, Alcibiades (c. 450-404 BCE), Athenian statesman, general. Alcibiades was recorded as being an effeminate aristocrat and an iconoclast. He married Hipparete, who left him as a result of his numerous infidelities (with women). Alcibiades was a successful warrior who often was in trouble for switching teams. He was murdered.

Alcibiades, along with others, officially contested Athenian democracy. This led to the trial (399) of Socrates for corrupting the morals of Athenian youth and for heresy (introducing strange gods). Socrates was found guilty and sentenced to death by drinking poisonous hemlock. Socrates left us nothing in writing. He is mostly known through the writings of his most famous student, Plato. In Plato's *The Symposium,* Socrates and Alcibiades speak of their thoughts and feelings of love, Alcibiades quite passionate about his adoration for old man Socrates.

HADRIAN AND ANTINOUS

Publius Aelius Hadrienus (January 24, 76-July 10, 138), Spanish-Roman emperor. Orphaned, Hadrian was adopted and mentored by the Roman Emperor Trajan, and ascended the throne in 117. Considered one of the great rulers of Rome, Hadrian traveled widely throughout his realm, conversing with leaders and wisepersons. He was well-liked for his patronage of the arts, development of infrastructure, inaugurating welfare for the poor, and enacting legislation against the mistreatment of slaves. He is responsible for Hadrian's Wall in England and for the reconstruction of the Pantheon (temple of all the gods) in Rome. Hadrian was married to Vibia Sabina.

Hadrian, Uffizi Gallery, Florence   Antinous

Hadrian was a pagan who worshipped goddesses and the phallus. He is also remembered for the death of 500,000 Jews who were banished from Jerusalem because they failed to enact Hadrian's new legislation forbidding the ritual of male genital mutilation (circumcision).

The love of Hadrian's life was Antinous (c. 110-October 130), Bithynian [Turkey]-Roman athlete. From the day they met (c. 124), Hadrian and Antinous were always together, until they went to Egypt and Antinous drowned in the Nile. Legend has it that Antinous heard an oracle prophesy Hadrian's premature death. So, to save the life of his lover and emperor, Antinous sacrificed himself to the river Nile at the age of nineteen. Hadrian never recovered from the loss of his intergenerational lover. Hadrian had festivals and a cult of Antinous inaugurated, coins minted in his honor, and cities named after him. Ironically, only a few statues of Emperor Hadrian remain, but more than 500 extant statues and busts of his romantic lover, Antinous, exist. Hadrian became grief-stricken and reclusive, retired to Rome, and died eight years after Antinous.

BIBLIOGRAPHY

Lambert, Royston (1984). *Beloved and God: The story of Hadrian and Antinous.* New York: Viking.

Yourcenar, Marguerite (1977). *Memoirs of Hadrian.* New York: Pocket Books.

RUMI AND SHAMS

Sweet moon without thy ray like a cloud I weep.

                                                    Rumi

Jalal ad-Din Rumi (1207-1273), Persian sage and poet mystic. As an Islamic preacher, Rumi founded the Mawlawiyya sect of the Sufi Order. In opposition to the growing orthodoxy of Islamic fundamentalism, in his religious teachings Rumi encouraged the exploration of passions and love. Rumi did not believe in waiting until after death for the reward of beauty, but instead advocated *shahid bazi,* the contemplation of God's beauty on Earth. Music and ecstatic dance were incorporated into this branch of Sufism—known in the West as the Whirling Dervishes—as a method to obtain divine inspiration. Although devoutly Islamic, Sufis are regarded as libertines who indulge in wine and hashish, and welcome blissful intoxications of love.

Shams al-Din (c. 1185-1248). Rumi met his older intergenerational lover Shams in 1244. The power and significance of their brief relationship affected their entire community and is evidenced by Rumi's many love poems to Shams. Rumi's wife, children, and disciples became increasingly jealous of Rumi's exclusive affections for Shams. Shams fled for his life, casting Rumi into great despair. Distraught by his father's lovesickness, Rumi's son Walad found Shams in Damascus and brought him home. Shams was soon murdered by Rumi's jealous pupils.

Rumi is entombed in Konya, Turkey.

SERGEI DIAGHILEV
AND VASLAV NIJINSKY

Sergei Pavlovich Diaghilev (March 19, 1872-August 19, 1929), Russian ballet impresario. A young Diaghilev moved in with his relatives in St. Petersburg (1890) to attend the Conservatory of Music. He soon became lovers with his cousin Dimitri "Dima" Filosofov. Dima took Diaghilev to his gymnasium, where he introduced his cousin to a wide circle of gay artists. Dima left Sergei (1904) for writer Zinaida Gippius.

Diaghilev was in Paris (1908) organizing a new company, the Ballets
Russe, when he met Vaslav Nijinsky (c.
February 28, 1890-April 8, 1950), Russian ballet dancer. At the time, Nijinsky
was living with his lover and benefactor, Prince Pavel Lvov. Diaghilev wran-
gled Nijinsky away and into his own
company. Nijinsky is considered one of
the greatest dancers of the twentieth
century. He was known for his jeté and
elevation. Most notable performances
of their shared celebrated careers are
*Petrouchka, Les Sylphides, Schéhéra-
zade, The Spectre of the Rose,* Stravinsky's *The Rite of Spring,* and Debussy's
The Afternoon of a Faun. The latter

Diaghilev and Nijinsky, 1923,
sketch by Jean Cocteau

caused a sensation when, on opening night (May 29, 1912) at Le
Théâtre du Chatelet in Paris, in what might be called "method dancing," Nijinsky was swept away enacting the faun and masturbated on
stage to orgasm.

   The dramatic and tempestuous intergenerational relationship of Diaghilev
and Nijinsky was notorious for its his-
trionics. They traveled together throughout the capitals of Europe, enjoying lav-
ish suites in the finest hotels. But
dressing rooms in opera houses filled
with bouquets and all the sybaritic caprices of which they indulged eventually tired Nijinsky. After five years with
Diaghilev, on a cruise to South America, Nijinsky fell in love with a Hungarian heiress and ballerina named Romola
de Pulszky. He left Diaghilev—in a
tragic Romeo-and-Juliet type misunder-
standing—and married Romola in Bue-
nos Aires (1913). Nijinsky soon began
to show signs of mental instability. He
last performed in 1917, and spent the

Vaslav Nijinsky, c. 1909

next thirty-three years in and out of mental institutions, with Romola caring for him. Nijinsky died and was buried in London, and exhumed three years later and reburied in Paris at Montmartre. Romola Nijinsky died in Paris in 1978.

Diaghilev had many future lovers, notably English dancer Anton Dolin, Russian dancer Serge Lifar, and Russian conductor Igor Markevitch. Diaghilev died and is buried in Venice, Italy, on the cemetery island of San Michele.

Sergei Diaghilev, c.1909

BIBLIOGRAPHY

Nijinsky, Romola (1980). *Nijinsky* and *The Last Years of Nijinsky*. New York: Simon & Schuster.

Percival, John (1971). *The World of Diaghilev*. New York: Harmony Books.

PAUL VERLAINE AND ARTHUR RIMBAUD

Although their stormy relationship lasted but a few brief years, it remains legendary in its poetry and passion. Paul Marie Verlaine (March 30, 1844-January 8, 1896), French poet. Verlaine established himself in the anti-Romantic new Parnassian movement with the publication of his first book of poetry (1866). Jean-Nicolas Arthur Rimbaud (October 20, 1854-November 10, 1891), French poet. The first of the Symbolists, at age sixteen Rimbaud sent copies of his poems to the famous Verlaine in Paris. Verlaine

Verlaine and Rimbaud, 1872. From the painting "Un coin de table" by Henri Fantin-Latour

was so impressed with Rimbaud's hallucinatory style that he invited Rimbaud to stay with him, his wife, son, and mother-in-law. It was not long before iconoclast Rimbaud was taciturn and contemptuous of the great poet Verlaine's bourgeois life.

They immediately fell in love, with sexual consummation. Adhering to a slovenly life of drunkenness and debauchery, Verlaine and Rimbaud were soon outcast from nonartistic circles as well as by Verlaine's wife, who sued for divorce.

Verlaine and Rimbaud were "happy vagabonds," incessantly traveling, drunk, and fighting their way through France, England, and Belgium. It was in Belgium (July 8, 1873) that Verlaine, histrionically despondent, got drunk, purchased a pistol, and fired three times at Rimbaud, hitting him once in the wrist. Rimbaud, fleeing to the train station, was accosted by Verlaine who, still in a drunken frenzy, made as if to shoot him again. This time Verlaine was arrested by the police. A week later the bullet was extracted and Rimbaud claimed in court that the shooting had been an accident. But at the trial, the doctor who had examined Verlaine in jail claimed that there was evidence on his body of both active and passive sodomy. Hmm. Verlaine was sentenced to two years at hard labor and fined 200 francs.

Rimbaud then abandoned poetry in pursuit of business opportunities (1879). He traveled extensively, and was often ill. In Africa and the Middle East (1888) Rimbaud established himself as an arms and ammunitions dealer. It is speculated that he may also have been involved in the lucrative slave trade. In severe ill health, Rimbaud returned to France where his leg was amputated. He died shortly thereafter at the age of thirty-seven.

Verlaine continued teaching, writing poetry, and living debauchedly. He was bisexual and had many lovers, notably student Lucien Létinois. Verlaine's life ended in a ménage à trois with two women: Philomène Boudin and Eugénie Krantz. He was buried in Paris at Batignolles Cemetery.

BIBLIOGRAPHY

Lehmann, John (1983). *Three Literary Friendships.* London: Quartet Books.

ANDRÉ GIDE AND MARC ALLÉGRET

Nothing of the past satisfies my love any longer. Everything in me blossoms forth; is amazed; my heart beats wildly; an excess of life rises to my throat like a sob. I no longer know anything; it is a vehemence without memories and without wrinkles . . .

André Gide
upon meeting Marc Allégret

Marc Allégret and André Gide in England, 1918

André Gide (né Paul Guillaume, November 22, 1869-February 19, 1951), French writer. Gide was suspended from school at age nine for masturbating. He married his cousin (1895), Madeleine Rondeaux. This romantic companionship was the focus of his earlier writings. Upon Gide's coming out (c. 1917), Mme. Gide burned his correspondence and later committed suicide. But it was with another woman that Gide fathered a daughter. He was astonishingly prolific, producing volumes of letters and journals, novels, and plays. His semi-autobiographical fiction includes *The Fruits of the Earth* (1897), *The Immoralist* (1902), *Strait Is the Gate* (1909), *Corydon* (1924), and *The Counterfeiters* (1926). Among his many awards, Gide was bestowed the Nobel Prize in Literature (1947).

By 1917, Gide was passionately in love with the son of a minister/friend (the friend having been the best man at Gide's wedding): Marc Allégret (December 23, 1900-November 3, 1973), Swiss film director, producer, screenwriter. Gide wrote on May 4, 1918: "Getting along without M. has already ceased to seem possible for me." Despite their age difference of thirty-one years, and the tempestuousness of their affairs and jealousies, their loving relationship was able to endure a remarkable thirty-four years. When they met, Allégret was fifteen and Gide was forty-seven. Their most legendary indiscretion is the tiff between Gide and **Jean Cocteau** over gaining the affections of Allégret. Gide took Allégret to England (June 18, 1918) for an extended holiday and to steal him away from the influence of Cocteau. Gide fictionalizes this account in his roman à clef, *The Counterfeiters*: Gide as Edouard, Cocteau as Passavant, Allégret as Olivier.

In 1925 Gide and Allégret traveled to the Congo. Allégret filmed much of their experience of the flora, fauna, and tribespeople, later selling these motion pictures in Paris. Allégret participated in the direction and/or production of more than fifty films, most notably directing *Lac aux Dames* (1930s). Allégret was interred in the Cimetière des Gonards in Versailles, France.

BIBLIOGRAPHY

Painter, George D. (1968). *Andre Gide: A Critical Biography*. New York: Atheneum.

Peters, Arthur King (1973). *Jean Cocteau and Andre Gide: An Abrasive Friendship*. New Jersey: Rutgers University Press.

Pollard, Patrick (1991). *Andre Gide: Homosexual Moralist*. London: Yale University Press.

JEAN COCTEAU AND RAYMOND RADIGUET

> Our initials interlaced
> in the sand, our bodies too:
> sooner than this moment
> will our love be erased.

> Raymond Radiguet
> (Radiguet, 1976, p. 33)

Jean Maurice Eugene Clement Cocteau (July 5, 1889-October 11, 1963), French poet, filmmaker, artist. Cocteau's long prolific life of artistry contributed to many media, most notably film: *Beauty and the Beast* (1946) and *Orpheus* (1950); novels: *The Terrible Children* (1929); nonfiction: *The White Paper* (1930). Cocteau also wrote poetry, plays, screenplays, was involved in opera and ballet, and was an actor, painter, set designer, and undoubtedly a beacon of creativity in France for half a century. Among his dozens of distinguished awards

Raymond Radiguet (standing) and Jean Cocteau, June 1922

and honors, Cocteau was elected to the Académie Française (c. 1955) and received the Commander of the Legion of Honor (1961).

Cocteau was almost as busy in his love life. He had many lovers, notably African-American boxer Al Brown (1935) and French actor Jean Marais (1937-1950). But it is said that the true love of his life was Raymond Radiguet (June 18, 1903-December 12, 1923), French poet, novelist. They met in 1918 when Radiguet was fifteen, and when Cocteau, twenty-nine, had just lost **Marc Allégret** to **André Gide.** Cocteau conceptualized his intergenerational relationship with Radiguet as a modern epic of French poets **Paul Verlaine** and **Arthur Rimbaud.** Cocteau later wrote: "Without RR I never would have reached perfection. . . . As soon as he came a way was opened in the direction of purity" (Brown, 1968, pp. 337-338).

Radiguet was a poet who reinvoked traditional style in an era of Bohemian, Dada, and post-Surrealist domination. His collection *Cheeks on Fire* (1921) was an instant national success. One evening Radiguet despairingly tossed the manuscript of his first novel into the fireplace (1922). Cocteau then locked him in his room until he rewrote his novel, best seller *The Devil in the Flesh* (1923).

Radiguet self-identified as bisexual and tormented Cocteau with his public displays of heterosexual courtship, notably with Bronca Pearlmutter. Cocteau followed his lover, passing him notes in cafés— ostensibly seeking reassurance of their love. A few days before his death from typhoid at age twenty, Radiguet told Cocteau, "In three days I shall be shot down by the soldiers of God" (Brown, 1968, p. 235). This great loss is supposedly what moved Cocteau into a deep depression and years of smoking opium. He wrote (1925), "I wanted to attain white whiter than snow and I saw how my instruments were smudged with nicotine. So I formed Radiguet to bring about, through him, what I could not do myself. . . . Now I am alone, stupefied with sorrow, standing amid the ruins of a crystal factory" (Brown, 1968, p. 237).

Jean Cocteau died the same day as bisexual French chanteuse Edith Piaf. Only four hours after offering his heartfelt praise of her life and soul on French Public Radio, Cocteau's heart stopped. He is buried at the Chapel of Saint Blaise des Simples, Milly.

Radiguet is buried in Paris at Père Lachaise.

BIBLIOGRAPHY

Brown, Frederick (1968). *An Impersonation of Angels: A Biography of Jean Cocteau.* New York: Viking Press.

Peters, Arthur King (1973). *Jean Cocteau and André Gide: An Abrasive Friendship.* New Jersey: Rutgers University Press.

Radiguet, Raymond (1976). *Cheeks on Fire: Collected Poems.* London: John Calder.

OSCAR WILDE AND LORD ALFRED DOUGLAS

To love oneself is the beginning of a lifelong romance.

Oscar Wilde
(Nicholls, 1980, p. 169)

Oscar Fingal O'Flahertie Wills Wilde (October 16, 1854-November 30, 1900), Irish wit, writer. Lord Alfred Bruce "Bosie" Douglas (October 22, 1870-March 20, 1945), Scottish nobleman, writer. Oscar and Bosie met in the summer of 1891. But their intergenerational relationship—"the love that dare not speak its name," (a phrasing of Bosie's often attributed to Wilde)—did not begin for another year. It is alleged that Bosie got himself into some homo-

Oscar Wilde and Lord Alfred Douglas at Oxford, 1894

sexual trouble at college, with a blackmailer, and so sought mentoring from the famous writer he'd met in London.

Before Wilde met Bosie, the Irish wit found early success as a poet and lecturer. During his famous American lecture tour (1882), he arrived in New York and proclaimed, "I have nothing to declare. Except my genius." "That, sir," the customs officer quipped, "is a commodity which does not require protection in the United States" (Nicholls, 1980, pp. 16-17). Wilde visited **Walt Whitman** and other manly comrades, but enjoyed San Francisco the most. Returning to London, Wilde married Constance Lloyd (1884) and had two sons. Constance was aware that Oscar had established a sexual relationship (1886) with gay Canadian Robbie Ross, creating an overlapping relationship. Ross remained Wilde's closest friend, confidant, executor of his estate, and lifetime rival of Bosie. Wilde's *The Happy Prince and Other Tales* (1888) was a celebrated homophile children's story of love and altruism between a statue and a swallow. His classic novel *The Picture of Dorian Gray* (1891) and his talk-of-the-town plays elevated Oscar Wilde to the scrutinized realm of celebrity.

Bosie was considered a very handsome lad. His aristocratic position was of interest to, but not exactly to the libidinal folly of, Oscar. Their interclass relationship was fraught with difficulty. Bosie found Oscar somewhat an embarrassment: fat, with bad teeth, and shamefully middle-class. Wilde's sexual appetite turned to "rough trade," working-class young men who would later get him into trouble. It is speculated that most of Oscar and Bosie's erotic pleasures were in the mutual pursuit of unreciprocated professional sex.

Bosie's macho father was the Marquess of Queensberry, a sportsman who gave his name to boxing's Queensberry Rules. He was a bully, an atheist, shunned from the House of Lords, considered insane by some, a real man's man who tried to toughen up his sons. When he moved his mistress into their home, his wife sued for divorce. At first, Bosie's father liked Oscar but he soon realized the queer rumors were true. He wrote to Wilde, calling him a "somdomite" *(sic)*. Bosie encouraged Wilde to sue for libel and then never testified on Wilde's behalf during the three ensuing trials. Wilde was found guilty of gross indecencies and sentenced to two years of hard labor (1895-1897). "Yet each man kills the thing he loves."

Broken-spirited, destitute, and in ill health, Oscar Wilde died in exile in Paris. Bosie and Ross gave him money and stayed by his side while most everyone else abandoned him. His magnificent tomb in Paris at Père Lachaise is well worth the visit. Bosie later married Olive Custance, and they produced a son, Raymond.

BIBLIOGRAPHY

Fido, Martin (1973). *Oscar Wilde.* New York: Viking.
Nicholls, Mark (1980). *The Importance of Being Oscar: The Life and Wit of Oscar Wilde.* New York: St. Martin's Press.

EDWARD CARPENTER AND GEORGE MERRILL

... there *is* an organic connection between the homosexual temperament and unusual psychic or divinatory powers.

Edward Carpenter
(Tsuzuki, 1980, p. 146)

Edward Carpenter (August 29, 1844-June 29, 1929), British writer, political activist, utopian, mystic. Carpenter was ordained a

George Merrill and Edward Carpenter

priest in the Anglican Church (1869) but soon quit (1874) for political, social, and religious reasons. He traveled the world studying Hinduism (becoming a vegetarian), Buddhism, and other expressions of spirituality. His anthropological studies of the Native American Two-Spirit (berdache), the Japanese samurai, and other global homoerotic traditions are documented in his *Intermediate Types Among Primitive Folk: A Study in Social Evolution* (1914). Carpenter visited his great American idol, poet **Walt Whitman** (1877 and 1884). In his bohemian life, counterculturist Carpenter wrote at least thirty volumes and more than 100 pamphlets on women's rights, socialism, prison reform and the justice system, vivisection and animal rights, male-male love, history, spirituality, and travel. Perhaps his most famous work is his book of poetry, *Toward Democracy* (1883).

Carpenter was a Fabian socialist who started a utopian society, Millthorpe, at Sheffield (1885), a community sustained by market gardening and sandal-making. George Merrill (c. 1869-January 1928) was a working-class young man, aimless, and looking lost in a train station when Carpenter picked him up (1889). They spent the rest of their lives together, working at Millthorpe, traveling, and protecting each other from the wrath of disapproving others. George Merrill was a strong worker, a dynamo, "fairly muscular"—and he had a nelly voice and gait, "intensely feminine." Merrill's unapologetic gender variance is among several issues that upset their straight socialist comrades, and precisely what Carpenter exalted in this "intermediate type." Their intergenerational relationship was musical: Carpenter played the piano and Merrill sang with his "beautiful voice." They are interred together. Although Carpenter was twenty-five years Merrill's senior, he buried his young lover before his own departure a year and a half later.

> . . . do not think too much of the dead husk of your friend, or mourn too much over it; but send your thoughts out toward the real soul or self which has escaped—to reach it. For so, surely, you will cast a light of gladness upon his onward journey, and contribute your part toward the building of that kingdom of love which links our earth to heaven.

> Edward Carpenter
> (Tsuzuki, 1980, p. 164)

BIBLIOGRAPHY

Tsuzuki, Chushichi (1980). *Edward Carpenter: Prophet of Human Fellowship.* London: Cambridge University Press.

KATHERINE BRADLEY AND EDITH COOPER

Katherine Harris Bradley (October 27, 1848-September 26, 1914), and Edith Emma Cooper (January 12, 1862-December 13, 1913), British poets, writers. Bradley, known most of her life as "Michael," was the aunt of Cooper, who was known most of her life as "Henry." The intergenerational relationship of Michael and Henry stirred up controversy in its gender-variant and incestuous nature. Neither woman ever married. They lived together their entire adult lives and wrote together under the pseudonym Michael Field. They were active in the women's suffrage movement and in campaigns against vivisection.

> There is love
> of woman unto woman, in its fibre
> Stronger than knits a mother to her child.
> There is no lack in it, and no defect;
> It looks nor up nor down,
> But loves from plenitude to plenitude.

(Grier and Reed, 1976, p. 30)

Katherine Bradley and Edith Cooper

W. H. AUDEN AND CHESTER KALLMAN

W. H. Auden

Who would complete without the
extra day
the journey that should take no time
at all?

Auden
(Auden, 1966, p. 179)

Wystan Hugh Auden (February 21, 1907-September 29, 1973), British-American poet. Auden was one of the most prolific writers of the twentieth century, and considered by some its greatest poet. Among his many awards were the Pulitzer Prize for "The Age of Anxiety" (1947), the National Medal for Literature (1967), and the National Book Award (1956). He was a stretcher-bearer for the Loyalists in the Spanish Civil War (1937). Auden was a close friend of writer **Christopher Isherwood,** with whom he traveled to China and co-authored the book *Journey to a War* (1938). Auden married (1935) writer Thomas Mann's daughter Erika as a means to provide her safe passage out of Nazi Germany. They were then divorced. Auden moved to the United States (1939) and became a citizen in 1946.

Three months after Auden arrived in the United States, he met and fell in love with Chester Simon Kallman (January 7, 1921-January 18, 1975), American librettist, companion. Auden and Kallman collaborated on many projects, including a dozen librettos, notably Igor Stravinsky's opera *The Rake's Progress* (1951). The intergenerational relationship of Auden and Kallman was sexually nonexclusive. They lived together for thirty-four years and wore gold wedding bands. Auden is buried in the Roman Catholic cemetery in Kirchstetten, Austria, outside of Vienna. Kallman is buried in the Jewish Cemetery in Athens.

BIBLIOGRAPHY

Auden, W. H. (1966). *Collected Shorter Poems.* London: Faber & Faber Ltd.
Farnan, Dorothy (1984). *Auden in Love.* New York: Simon & Schuster.

CHRISTOPHER ISHERWOOD AND DON BACHARDY

Don Bachardy and Christopher Isherwood

Christopher William Bradshaw Isherwood (August 26, 1904-January 4, 1986), British-American writer. Isherwood's legendary literary career began at about the time his intergenerational lover was born. Living in Berlin, Isherwood chronicled his life in pre-Nazi Germany in his book *The Berlin Stories* (1946), later made into the movie *Cabaret* (1972). Isherwood also wrote plays, screenplays, translations, memoirs *(Christopher and His Kind,* 1976), and a treatise on his longtime relationship with Swami Prabhavananda and Vedantic Hinduism, *My Guru and His Disciple* (1980). Isherwood often wrote in the third person about his life as an out-of-the-closet gay man. He promoted frank discussions of a positive gay identity and the imperative need for a gay community, which he referred to as his "tribe." Isherwood collaborated with homofriendly heterosexual psychologist and sex researcher Evelyn Hooker.

In 1953 Isherwood, forty-nine, met the love of his life, Don Bachardy (c. 1935--), American painter. Around 1960, with Isherwood's encouragement and support, Bachardy attended art school at Chouinard. Bachardy has spent most of his luminous career painting portraits of famous persons, notably California Governor Jerry Brown, whose Bachardy portrait hangs in the capitol building in Sacramento.

The thirty-three-year intergenerational relationship of Isherwood and Bachardy was sexually nonexclusive. They lived together in Santa Monica. Bachardy still resides in the same home. Isherwood's archives are at the Huntington Library in Pasadena, and he donated his body to science at UCLA.

BIBLIOGRAPHY

Berg, James and Freeman, Christopher (2000). *The Isherwood Century: Essays on the Life and Work of Christopher Isherwood.* Madison: University of Wisconsin.

TENNESSEE WILLIAMS AND FRANK MERLO

Merlo and Williams at St. Mark's Square, Venice, 1948

Tennessee (né Thomas Lanier) Williams (March 26, 1911-February 25, 1983), American writer. Williams wrote short stories, novels, poetry, memoirs, and screenplays, but is best remembered for his seventy plays and is considered by many the greatest American playwright of the twentieth century. His most notable plays are *The Glass Menagerie* (1944), Pulitzer Prize–winning *A Streetcar Named Desire* (1947), *Summer and Smoke* (1948), Pulitzer Prize–winning *Cat on a Hot Tin Roof* (1955), *Suddenly Last Summer* (1958), and *The Night of the Iguana* (1961).

In Provincetown, MA (July 1947), Williams met the love of his life, Frank Philip Merlo (c. 1922-

Merlo and Williams at Key West

Williams and Merlo at South Beach

1963), American companion. After six years of serving in the U.S. Navy, Merlo left his lover, lyricist John LaTouche, for Williams. They consummated their fresh union in the sand dunes of Cape Cod. Their intergenerational relationship was sexually nonexclusive. Williams openly referred to his hunky lover of Italian descent as "Little Horse." When asked by movie mogul Jack Warner, "And what do you do?" Merlo replied, "I sleep with Mr. Williams."

It is reported that Merlo suffered contempt from some of Williams' friends and associates. But most people attest to Merlo's unwavering devotion to Williams and to attending to Williams' large public life. Merlo's closest lifetime friend, actress Maureen Stapleton, said of Frankie, ". . . everyone loved him . . . And he loved and protected Tenn and did everything for him" (Spotto, 1985, p. 170). But as Williams' fame and wealth grew, Merlo's role became more ambiguous. After fourteen years together they broke up (1962).

Merlo, who had smoked four packs of cigarettes a day, died of lung cancer in 1963. Williams deteriorated on all levels over the next twenty years. He died in a hotel room from having choked on a bottle cap, and was interred in the Cavalry Cemetery, St. Louis.

BIBLIOGRAPHY

Spotto, Donald (1985). *The Kindness of Strangers: The Life of Tennessee Williams.* Boston: Little, Brown & Company.

Sara Teasdale

SARA TEASDALE
AND MARGARET CONKLIN

There are so many ways to love
And each way has its own delight—
Then be content to come to me
Only as spray the beating sea
Drives inland through the night.

Sara Teasdale
(Teasdale, 1920)

Sarah Trevor Teasdale (August 8, 1884-January 29, 1933), American poet. Teasdale was shy and introverted, and severely depressed most of her life. Her lyric style of poetry focused on themes of love, notably Sapphic love. Teasdale's volumes of poetry include *Sonnets to Duse and Other Poems* (1907), *Helen of Troy* (1911), *Love Songs* (1917), *Flame and Shadow* (1920), and *Dark of the Moon* (1926). She was awarded the Poetry Society Award and the Columbia University Poetry Society (Pulitzer) Prize (1918).

Her marriage (1914-1929) was childless, Teasdale having terminated her one pregnancy. She had entered her marriage with great hopes and passion for a perfect romantic life, but became disillusioned and seriously depressed.

Margaret Conklin (c. 1903-c. 1984), American writer, bohemian. Conklin wrote a fan letter to Teasdale—who usually did not answer her mail—but something in Conklin's letter was significant enough to establish their epistolary relationship, which evolved into one of intergenerational lovers. Teasdale's poetry of tragic love turned to a positive note after she met Conklin (October 1926) and began dedicating poems to her. They traveled to Europe together (1927). They maintained separate residences; Conklin, living in her lower East Side tenement with bohemian artist friends, went daily to visit the recluse Teasdale in her Central Park West apartment.

Teasdale's depression eventually overpowered her and she committed suicide with an overdose of sleeping pills. She named Margaret Conklin as her heir and literary executor. Teasdale's ashes are buried in a family plot at Bellefontaine Cemetery, in her native St. Louis.

BIBLIOGRAPHY

Drake, William, "Sara Teasdale: Poet of love reborn in friendship." *New York Times: Book Review,* c. 1984.

Teasdale, Sara (1920). *Flame and Shadow.* New York: MacMillan Co.

MARTINA NAVRATILOVA
AND RITA MAE BROWN

Martina Navratilova (October 18, 1956–), Czechoslovakian-American tennis champion, activist. Navratilova defected from her native land (1975) and became a United States citizen (1981). She is perhaps the greatest champion in the history of women's tennis. Navratilova has been consistently outspoken about her lesbianism and her opinions about gay rights, the only major athlete to do so continuously for three decades. Her financial sacrifices and longevity of lesbian visibility are remarkable.

Rita Mae Brown (November 28, 1944–), American writer, political activist. Brown is the author of more than forty novels, most notably *Rubyfruit Jungle* (1973). Her work is known for its Southern grace, charm, and bawdy humor. Rita Mae was a founding member of the National Organization for Women, the Redstockings collective (1969), the Furies (1971-1973), and many other lesbian, gay, and women's groups. She has also consistently been an outspoken lesbian and role model for gay and lesbian youth. Brown is noted romantically for her passionate serial monogyny.

The celebrated romance of Brown and Navratilova was passion-filled and short-lived (1979-1981). The gossip never ceases for these two legendary lesbians and their intergenerational quirky karma. Brown's roman à clef about a famous lesbian tennis star, *Sudden Death* (1983), added fuel to the fire. Brown was quoted, "When my mother met Martina, she said, 'Honey, have a child, don't marry one.'" In the small incestuous world of A-lesbians, Martina's lover Judy Nelson split from her to shack up with Rita Mae at her Virginian horse farm. Nelson then sued Navratilova for "galimony" and, it is reported, received a multimillion-dollar settlement. Stay tuned. There's bound to be more from these legendary lesbian lovers.

BIBLIOGRAPHY

Bonk, Thomas, "Jumping into retirement." *Los Angeles Times*, July 31, 1994.

Mansfield, Stephanie, "The love match gone sour." *Washington Post*, August 13, 1981.

Rosenfield , Paul, "Gay feminist rubs shoulders in prime time." *Datebook*, March 14, 1982.

Witteman, Paul A., "Last waltz at Wimbledon." *Time*, July 11, 1994.

RUTH BENEDICT AND MARGARET MEAD

What is new is not bisexuality but rather the widening of our awareness and acceptance of human capacities for sexual love.

Margaret Mead
(Howard, 1984, p. 367)

Ruth Fulton Benedict (June 5, 1887-September 17, 1948) and Margaret Mead (December 16, 1901-November 15, 1978), American anthropologists. Benedict and Mead were trailblazers in their field of science. They both discarded their predecessors' shame of sexuality by studying and documenting the sexual orientations and gender identification constructions of "primitive folk." Together and independently they challenged the homophobia of psychology and medicine in Western science.

Benedict, born into a well-educated but impoverished family, was hearing disabled and suffered from a variety of emotional pathologies. Nevertheless, she graduated from Vassar College (1909) Phi Beta Kappa, and earned her PhD in anthropology at Columbia University (1923) under the tutelage of Franz Boas. Her marriage to Stanley Benedict (1914) was childless, not a match made in heaven, and by the mid-1920s they were spending only weekends together. Their union ended (1930) with neither remarrying. Benedict was studying Indians of the Southwest and penning under the name

"Anne Singleton." She wrote many texts, most notably *Patterns of Culture* (1934), *Zuni Mythology* (1935), and *The Chrysanthemum and the Sword: Patterns of Japanese Culture* (1946). Other loves of her life were research chemist Natalie Raymond (1931-1939) and Ruth Valentine (1939-1948).

Mead was raised by agnostic intellectual parents. She achieved much fame and notoriety in her life with the publication of her controversial *Coming of Age in Samoa* (1928). Many of her volumes are about human sexuality, but better known are (autobiography) *Blackberry Winter* (1972), and (with **James Baldwin**) *A Rap on Race* (1971). Mead was married three times and divorced twice, producing one daughter, and she had many female lovers in between.

Ruth Benedict, 1924

Margaret Mead, 1925

Professor Benedict and student Mead met at Barnard College in 1922. Their passionate, if brief, intergenerational mentor/lover relationship was a foundation for decades of scientific collaboration.

BIBLIOGRAPHY

Howard, Jane (1984). *Margaret Mead: A Life.* New York: Simon & Schuster.

GEORGE WASHINGTON CARVER AND AUSTIN W. CURTIS JR.

George Washington Carver, 1906

Austin W. Curtis Jr., February 27, 1940

Dr. George Washington Carver (c. 1864-January 5, 1943), American agricultural chemist. Carver was born a slave in Missouri to an abolitionist household. He was kidnapped and later abandoned. Carver graduated from Iowa State College (BS, 1894; MA, 1896). At Tuskegee Institute, Carver was named Director of the Department of Agriculture Research (1896).

Carver dedicated his life to bettering the existence of black Americans. He taught soil improvement and crop rotation, invented 300 uses for peanuts (e.g., peanut butter), and invented products from cotton waste. His birthplace was made into a national monument (1953). Carver never married, and was reported to have a decidedly feminine voice.

In 1935, Carver met Austin Wingate Curtis Jr., American scientist. Curtis graduated from Cornell University (1932). Carver and Curtis lived and traveled together. In this intergenerational relationship, Carver was mentor to Curtis, and then Curtis cared for Carver in his old age.

BIBLIOGRAPHY

Kremer, Gary R. (1987). *George Washington Carver: In His Own Words.* Columbia: University of Missouri Press.

Neyland, James (1991). *George Washington Carver: Scientist and Educator.* Los Angeles: Melrose Square Publishing.

MARY WOOLLEY AND JEANNETTE MARKS

My own Darling, the year has brought me no gift as great as
your love.

Miss Woolley to Miss Marks, 1900
(Wells, 1978, p. 61)

Mary Emma Woolley (July 13, 1863-September 5, 1947) and
Jeannette Augustus "Gussie" Marks (August 16, 1875-Spring 1964),
American educators. Miss Woolley and Miss Marks were a couple
for more than fifty years. Their intergenerational relationship began
at Wellesley College (1895) when Miss Marks was a student in Miss
Woolley's Biblical History class.

Woolley, the first woman to graduate from Brown University
(1894), was the president of Mount Holyoke College for thirty-six
years. She was an ardent advocate of world peace and a delegate at
the Disarmament Conference in Geneva (1931). Marks was the chair-
man of the Department of English Literature at Mount Holyoke and
the author of twenty books.

Mary Woolley and Jeannette Marks at Fluer de Lys

BIBLIOGRAPHY

Wells, Anna Mary (1978). *Miss Marks and Miss Woolley*. New York: Houghton Mifflin Company.

WALT WHITMAN AND PETER DOYLE

Walter Whitman (May 31, 1819-March 26, 1892), American poet, prophet of love. Considered by most academic scholars of literature to be the most important poet in American history, Walt Whitman freed himself from the confines of poetic meter and created "free verse." He added to and reedited his main body of work, *Leaves of Grass*, several times throughout his long and celebrated life. This collection contains passages that are explicitly sexual and homoerotic—a bold proclamation for the 1850s—most notably, "Song of Myself," "I Sing the Body Electric," and poems from the "Calamus" section.

Whitman made his living as a journalist, expounding on his favorite topics: politics, American workers, nature, industrialization, justice, and equality. During the Civil War, Walt volunteered as a "wound dresser" in an army hospital in Washington City (DC), caring for the dying, holding their hands and kissing them, writing letters home for the illiterate. With his manly gait, his robust voice and hearty laugh, his intentionally plebeian attire, serene blue eyes, and long fluffy beard, Whitman was fully conscious of creating his public image as the "good, gray poet," in his mission to advocate for "the dear love of comrades."

Walt Whitman and Peter Doyle, 1865

People from all over America and Europe made pilgrimages to meet the great American bard, notably celebrated homosexuals **Oscar Wilde** ("There is no one in this great wide world of America whom I love and honor so much" [Shively, 1987, p. 10]), **Edward Carpenter,** and John

Addington Symonds. Symonds annoyed Whitman with his vehement requests that Walt "come out" as a homosexual two years before Walt's death. Whitman replied: ". . . that the calamus part has even allow'd the possibility of such construction as mention'd is terrible" (p. 25). Whitman's most common erotic impulse was toward young working-class men, most of whom were sexually exploratory prior to marriage. Any social construction that would have divided gay men and straight men was anathema to Whitman's essential belief that all men should love one another.

Of Whitman's scores of intergenerational relationships, biographers concur that the most "adhesive love" was that of Peter George Doyle (c. 1847-1907), Irish-American horsecar conductor. Doyle's family immigrated to Virginia, where he was later captured as a Confederate soldier. Doyle and Whitman (who had twenty-eight years between them) met in Washington City toward the end of the Civil War one stormy night. Walt had a penchant for teamsters and often rode public transportation for entertainment. Doyle was a two-dollar-a-day omnibus driver, illiterate, and possibly manic depressive. They rode alone most of the night and fell in love at first sight. Doyle recalled forty years later: "We were familiar at once—I put my hand on his knee—we understood. He did not get out at the end of the trip—in fact went all the way back with me" (Shively, 1987, p. 100).

Whitman tutored Doyle in reading and writing, reciting poetry to him during their long walks and rides together. Doyle later became a railroad baggage handler, never quite attaining financial security; Whitman often sent him cash. This mentoring relationship worked both ways. Doyle was a frequenter of gay establishments and the burgeoning community. He also was more ambulatory than his sage companion.

Whitman had a fascinating relationship with President Lincoln (although they never met). Doyle was at Ford's Theater when Lincoln was assassinated and was henceforth requested by Whitman to recount every minute detail over and over.

They remained good friends and epistolary companions until Walt's death. Whitman wrote of Doyle:

> I never met a man that seemed to me, as far as I could tell in 40 minutes, more open, coarse, self-willed, strong, and free from the sickly desire to be on society's lines and points. (Shively, 1987, p. 56)

And said Doyle of Whitman:

> Walt often spoke to me of his books. I would tell him, "I don't know what you are trying to get at." And this is the idea I would always arrive at from his reply. All other peoples in the world have had their representatives in literature: here is a great big race with no representative. He would undertake to furnish that representative. It was also his object to get a real human being into a book. These were the two things he tried to impress upon me every time we talked of books—especially of his books. (Shively, 1987, p. 118)

Walt Whitman is buried in a tomb of his design in Harleigh Cemetery, Camden, New Jersey. Peter Doyle died in Philadelphia, and is buried with his brother in Washington, DC, at the Congressional Cemetery at 18th and E Streets (S.E.).

BIBLIOGRAPHY

Barton, William E. (1928). *Abraham Lincoln and Walt Whitman.* Indianapolis: The Bobbs-Merrill Company.

Elliot, Charles N. (1915). *Walt Whitman As a Man, Poet and Friend: Being Autograph Pages from Many Pens.* Boston: The Gorham Press.

Ferris, Haviland, "Portrait of the Young Man as Friend of the Poet," *Washington Blade,* March 20, 1981.

Kaplan, Justin (1980). *Walt Whitman: A Life.* New York: Simon and Schuster.

Shively, Charley (1987). *Calamus Lovers: Walt Whitman's Working Class Camerados.* San Francisco: Gay Sunshine Press.

Shively, Charley (1989). *Drum Beats: Walt Whitman's Civil War Boy Lovers.* San Francisco: Gay Sunshine Press.

MALCOLM BOYD AND MARK THOMPSON

What a difference thirty years can make. Time enough for two major wars, a worldwide depression, and more popular culture than anyone would care to remember. Thirty years—our age difference—the span that separates me and you.

Thompson to Boyd
(Lassell and Schimel, 1997, p. 32)

Malcolm Boyd (June 8, 1923–), American priest, author, activist. Born to a wealthy Manhattan couple who lost their fortune during the stock market crash, Boyd and his mother relocated to Colorado where Malcolm soothed his loneliness by reading, writing, and listening to the New York Metropolitan Opera broadcasts. He graduated from the University of Arizona (1944), and moved to Los Angeles where he was employed first in advertising and then in the film industry, where his fortunes quickly rose. Soon he became a business partner and lifelong friend of movie icon Mary Pickford. Boyd chose to leave his glamorous Hollywood life behind in order to become an Episcopal priest (1951).

Malcolm Boyd and Mark Thompson at home in Silverlake, 1988

Years of study and world travel followed, as did the first of more than thirty books, notably, *Are You Running with Me, Jesus?* (1965). This book was a sensational success, selling more than one million copies, turning Malcolm into an international celebrity. He risked his life to serve as a Freedom Rider (1961) in the segregated South and subsequently marched with Martin Luther King Jr. Boyd was the first ordained American priest to publicly come out as a gay man (1976), garnering him the cover of *Look* magazine.

Years of isolation were to follow until he met (1984) his intergenerational life partner of more than twenty years now. Mark Howard Thompson (August 19, 1952–), American author, photographer, historian, spiritualist. Born and raised in the sylvan paradise of Monterey, California, Thompson struggled to find meaning in life within a childhood of challenging family issues. He moved to San Francisco (1973), where he graduated from San Francisco State University with a degree in journalism, and was a features writer and cultural affairs editor at *The Advocate* for nineteen years. His books include *Gay Spirit: Myth and Meaning* (1987), *Gay Soul: Finding the Heart of Gay Spirit and Nature* (1994), *Gay Body: A Journey*

Through Shadow to Self (1997), *Leatherfolk: Radical Sex, People, Politics and Practice* (1991), and *Long Road to Freedom* (1994; edited). He has penned numerous essays, and created a traveling photo exhibition delineating gay history and culture.

Thompson was in Los Angeles on assignment for *The Advocate* to interview the legendary gay couple **Christopher Isherwood** and **Don Bachardy** when he met Boyd. In an uncanny premonition of things to come, the age difference between the famous writer (Isherwood) and his artist partner (Bachardy)—three decades—is the same age difference between Boyd and Thompson. On May 16, 2004, their intergenerational union was officially blessed by the Right Reverend J. Jon Bruno in Los Angeles' Cathedral Center of St. Paul. It was the first same-sex blessing by a seated Episcopal Bishop in the history of the United States.

> I realize how thankful I am for your life, how precious our time together is, and what an extraordinary adventure we have embarked upon. I am astonished by its mystery and pragmatism, awesomeness, and simple joy. I wouldn't have missed loving you for all the world.
>
> Boyd to Thompson
> (Lassell and Schimel, 1997, p. 36)

BIBLIOGRAPHY

Lassell, Michael and Schimel, Lawrence (eds.) (1997). *Two Hearts Desire: Gay Couples on Their Love.* New York: St. Martin's Press.

Chapter 3

Pattern of Overlapping Love

> The chains of marriage are heavy and it takes two to carry them, sometimes three.
>
> Oscar Wilde
> (Fisher, 1992, p. 171)

Overlapping love is a romantic relationship of two or more people, wherein one or both partners acquire additional partner(s) while primary partners retain loyalty. Overlapping love is usually manifested in a domestic alliance, such as a ménage à trois (household of three), and does not consist of short-term affairs or infatuations. These are committed relationships of more than two queer persons.

The sexualities of overlapping lovers vary, and in most of these romantic constellations the nature of the sexual relationships of those involved is indiscernible. It appears as though many of these relationships started off being sexual in a certain way, and then changed throughout time and partnerships. The aspect of importance here is that the original two lovers felt compelled to stay together, even when their lives took an unexpected turn in the road.

This love style ain't for everyone. It takes strongly developed individuals who are capable of adequately processing their jealousy. Overlapping lovers are generally people who host a creativity and courage to pioneer a relationship outside the confines of normality.

Legacies of Love: A Heritage of Queer Bonding
© 2008 by The Haworth Press, Taylor & Francis Group. All rights reserved.
doi:10.1300/5890_04

ALEXANDER THE GREAT AND HEPHAESTION AND BAGOAS

Alexander III (356-June 323 BCE), King of Macedon, conqueror. Alexander the Great has remained legendary in Western history for 2,300 years as one of the most successful warriors of all time. Son of Philip II, King of Macedon, and Olympias, Alexander maintained a devotional relationship to his mother, especially when his father took a new, favored wife. Alexander was tutored by Athenian scholar Aristotle.

Upon the murder of his father, Alexander, age twenty, ascended the throne (336 BCE). Alexander suppressed insurrection and began his campaign to conquer Persia on his famed horse, Boukephalos. Alexander took with him his boyhood friend and lover, Hephaestion, (c. 356-324 BCE), Macedonian warrior. When they arrived in Troy, Alexander ceremoniously placed a wreath at the tomb of Achilles while Hephaestion placed a wreath at the tomb of Patroclus.

Alexander the Great

Hephaestion is described as being taller, darker, and more handsome than Alexander. Alexander is sometimes described as a slightly effeminate dandy fond of fine foreign clothing. Alexander worshipped the goddess Artemis, and was known to dress as her in parades. He had many wives (the most notable being Roxana), most of whom were princesses of conquered nations. He ordered thousands of his soldiers to marry Persian women after the conquest. But Alexander spent very little time with his wives, preferring the company of male slave youths and *megabyzoi*—Persian gender-variant eunuchs. In her novel *The Persian Boy*, **Mary Renault** chronicles the legend of Alexander's great love for his favorite *megabyzoi*, Bagoas.

On campaign in Babylon, Hephaestion became feverish and unexpectedly died. Alexander's grief was insurmountable. In what Renault described as the most spectacular funeral in history, Alexander had the attending physician crucified, walls of neighboring towns torn down, all horses' manes cut, forbade music, and set 10,000 men to building a tomb. Alexander never recovered from his loss. In less than a year he, too, caught a fever and died within ten days at the age of thirty-three.

LEONARDO DA VINCI AND SALAI
AND FRANCESCO MELZI

Leonardo da Vinci (April 15, 1452-May 2, 1519), Italian genius. Da Vinci was an architect, engineer, inventor, sculptor, mathematician, and artist who rarely finished any project. Few of his works and sketches have survived, notably (of his eighteen paintings) the *Mona Lisa* and *The Last Supper.*

Along with three other young artists, charges were brought against da Vinci in the 1476 trial of a seventeen-year-old male prostitute, Jacopo Saltarelli. Da Vinci was acquitted.

In 1490, Leonardo met and adopted Salai (né Gian Giacomo Caprotti, c. 1480-unknown), Italian thief, voluptuary. Although Salai ("little devil") was only ten at the onset of their intergenerational relationship, he and da Vinci lived and traveled together for almost thirty years. In 1506, Leonardo met and adopted Francesco Melzi (c. 1488-1570), Italian nobleman, who joined Leonardo and Salai in an overlapping relationship for seven years. The majority of Leonardo's estate was split between his two lovers, with Melzi as the executor.

BIBLIOGRAPHY

"Leonardo Goes Straight for CBS: Better Heresy Than Homosexuality?" *The Advocate,* September 27, 1972.

Payne, Robert (1978). *Leonardo.* New York: Doubleday & Company, Inc.

Russo, William R., "Leonardo, a brush with gayness," *In Touch.*

ELEANOR BUTLER AND SARAH PONSONBY AND MARTHA CARYLL

Lady Eleanor Charlotte Butler (1739-June 2, 1828), and Sarah Ponsonby (1755-1830), Irish ladies of leisure. Volumes of journals and reams of correspondence attest to the passionate relationship of Butler and Ponsonby. Ponsonby was sent to a boarding school upon being orphaned, where, at thirteen, she first met Butler, twenty-nine (1768). Their intergenerational relationship spanned over half of a century.

Artistic renderings of Sarah Ponsonby and Eleanor Butler

Both women were born into affluent aristocratic families who fully expected to find suitable husbands for their heiresses. Word got out of their "romantic friendship," and their families separated them. Not a problem for butch Eleanor and femme Sarah: they eloped. Unfortunately they were caught and returned, Butler actually spending time in jail. However, Butler's bull-dyke maid, Martha Caryll, (aka Molly the Bruiser, unknown-November 1809), passed forbidden letters between Ponsonby and Butler. This facilitated their second, successful elopement. All three ran away together and lived happily ever after. They are buried together.

Ponsonby and Butler were notorious in their time for their charm, civility, and kindnesses. Their lives consisted of gardening, reading and writing, entertaining, painting with watercolor, and having tea. Their families finally agreed to provide them with financial independence if they stayed in Wales.

BIBLIOGRAPHY

Mavor, Elizabeth (1971). *The Ladies of Llangollen: A Study in Romantic Friendship*. London: Penguin Books.

RADCLYFFE HALL AND LADYE BATTEN AND UNA TROUBRIDGE AND EVGUENIA SOULINE

Marguerite Radclyffe Hall (August 12, 1880-October 7, 1943), British novelist, poet, and author of short stories. Hall was raised sometimes as a boy, and was known most of her life as "John." By 1906, John was writing poetry explicit with same-gender love. However, it was her novel *The Well of Loneliness* (1928) and its subsequent banning in England and the United States that garnered Hall a place in literary immortality. The first edition of *The Well of Loneliness* contains an introduction by British sexologist **Havelock Ellis.** Some contemporary lesbian critics feel that Hall's earlier lesbian-themed novel *The Unlit Lamp* (1924) is a better novel, although it has received less acclaim.

Lady Una Vincenzo Troubridge (March 8, 1887-September 24, 1963), British opera singer, sculptor, translator. In 1915, Troubridge

Una Troubridge and Radclyffe Hall with dachshunds

left her daughter and admiral husband when butch and suave John
swept her off her feet at a tea. This happened even though John,
thirty-five, was still in an intergenerational relationship (1908-1916)
with Mabel Veronica "Ladye" (née Hatch) Batten, fifty-eight. Una
joined John and (her cousin) Ladye in an overlapping relationship.
Una translated from the French, Italian, and Russian languages and
was the first to translate **Colette** into English.

Both Hall and Troubridge were stunningly beautiful women in
their earlier years. They practiced occult sciences and enjoyed many
years of showing dogs. They were well-known for their manly attire,
often accompanied by monocles. Troubridge remained devoted to
Hall for twenty-eight years until the latter's death, even though after
nineteen years of apparent monogamy, Hall took another lover,
Evguenia Souline, who moved in with them in another overlapping
relationship.

Ladye and John are buried together at Highgate Cemetery in London. Una's burial instructions to be interred with John and Ladye
were not discovered until after she was buried at the Protestant Cemetery in Rome. Una had a plaque installed at John's crypt, which reads:

Radclyffe Hall

And, if God choose
I shall but love thee better
after death.
Una

BIBLIOGRAPHY

Baker, Michael (1985). *Our Three Selves: A Life of Radclyffe Hall.* Vale, Guernsey, British Channel Islands: Guernsey Press.

Brittain, Vera (1968). *Radclyffe Hall: A Case of Obscenity?* London: Femina.

Dickson, Lovat (1975). *Radclyffe Hall at the Well of Loneliness: A Sapphic Chronicle.* New York: Charles Scribners & Sons.

Ormrod, Richard (1985). *Una Troubridge: The Friend.* New York: Carroll & Graf Publishers, Inc.

S. JOSEPHINE BAKER AND I. A. R. WYLIE AND LOUISE PEARCE

Sara Josephine Baker (November 15, 1873-February 22, 1945), American physician, public health administrator, child health pioneer. Young Josephine, a wild tomboy, was sent to Misses Thomas' finishing school. After earning her MD (1898) Baker went into private practice in New York City, but found a bigger calling: she was the first American woman to receive a doctorate in Public Health (1917). Dr. Baker was instrumental in creating and heading many public health committees in New York, greatly improving the quality of life for children.

S. Josephine Baker

She was often quoted as saying, "It's six times safer to be a soldier in the trenches of France than to be born a baby in the United States." She is also responsible for identifying "Typhoid Mary." Dr. Baker never married. She cross-dressed, wearing tailored suits and neckties, and rimless pince-nez. Beginning in the 1920s, she lived in New York City with her intergenerational lover, I. A. R. Wylie.

Ida Alexa Ross Wylie (March 16, 1885-November 4, 1959), Australian-American popular novelist, screenwriter, traveler. Born of Scottish parents in Australia, Wylie was three when her family migrated from Melbourne to London. She was educated in Belgium and Germany, and traveled Europe as an independent child, venturing solo to Norway at age twelve. Wylie was twenty when her first novel was published. Notable of her more than a dozen novels are *The Silver Virgin* (1929), *The Young in Heart* (1938), and *Keeper of the Flame* (1942). Her memoir, *My Life with George* (1940), chronicles her twenty years with Baker. Wylie made several trips to Hollywood to work on screenplays. She was self-described as a "militant suffragist." Two of her books are dedicated "with love" to "L. P."

Louise Pearce (1885-1959), American physician, researcher. Dr.

Louise Pearce

Pearce completed her undergraduate degree in science at Stanford University, and received her medical degree from Johns Hopkins. At age thirty-five she traveled alone to Zaire to study the effects of a new drug on sleeping sickness. For this act of courage Pearce was awarded in Belgium the Royal Order of Lion and The Royal Order of the Crown. She was a lifelong associate of the Rockefeller Institute of Medical Research.

In their overlapping relationship, Baker, Wylie, and Pearce together purchased Trevenna Farm, a 200-year-old homestead in Belle Mead, New Jersey, where they shared their love and lives.

H.D. AND BRYHER AND KENNETH MACPHERSON

H.D. and Bryher

This one's a little tricky, so let me start with a synopsis: Wealthy lesbian falls in love with bisexual woman who needs to also have a man, so they get one. He marries the lesbian (lover of his lover) and adopts his bisexual lover's daughter, thereby making both of her adoptive parents the lovers of her biological mother.

Hilda Doolittle (September 10, 1886-September 27, 1961), American poet, novelist, translator. H.D. led a passionate life of ups and downs. When she was fifteen, H.D. met Ezra Pound, sixteen, at a costume party. They fell in love and became engaged, but never married. H.D.'s first significant love relationship instead was with friend Frances Gregg. Pound encouraged H.D. in her Imagist poetry with its strong foundation in classic Greek. Her first collection, *Sea Garden* (1916) garnered instant acclaim. H.D. had a romantic attachment to writer D. H. Lawrence, and married poet Richard Aldington (1913), who left her for another woman (1917).

Bryher (née Annie Winifred Ellerman, September 2, 1894-January 28, 1983), British writer, heiress. Bryher, born into one of England's wealthiest families, was heiress to a shipping fortune. She was a writer of poetry, novels, fiction, and memoirs, notably *The Heart to Artemis* (1962). Bryher was starstruck by H.D.'s poetry when they met (1918). The rest of their lives were spent together in a variety of forms: lovers, companions, and travel partners, with Bryher as H.D.'s benefactor.

But like most couples, H.D. and Bryher had issues. To help resolve their complicated needs, these legendary women sought the counseling of sexologist **Havelock Ellis.** H.D. was an avowed bisexual, and although she adored making love with Bryher, she also craved sex with men and male companionship. Bryher was a manic and possessive lover, and could not bear to lose her little woman. Ellis suggested

Kenneth Macpherson and Bryher at Spitzbergen, 1929

that they bring a man into their relationship. The man was Kenneth Macpherson.

Bryher had married bisexual American writer Robert McAlmon (1921-1927) as a means to acquiring access to her family's financial interests. Bryher later married (1927-1947) H.D.'s lover, Kenneth Macpherson, constructing an overlapping relationship of ménage à trois. Bryher and Macpherson then adopted (1927) H.D.'s daughter Perdita (fathered by ex-lover Cecil Gray). Poor Perdita was sent away to boarding schools; however, she did become sole heir to her mother's lover's fortune. The overlapping relationship of these three lasted for twenty years; they spent most of their time in Switzerland. They made three movies together, notably *Borderline* (1930) with Paul and Eslanda Robeson. In this film, Bryher cross-dressed as a cigar-smoking innkeeper.

BIBLIOGRAPHY

Gilbert, Sandra M., "A Globe-Trotting Literary Flapper," *Review,* May 13, 1984.
Guest, Barbara (1984). *Herself Defined: The Poet H.D. and Her World.* New York: Doubleday and Company, Inc.

FRANKLIN AND ELEANOR ROOSEVELT AND LUCY MERCER AND LORENA HICKOK

Goodnight, dear one. I want to put my arms around you and kiss you at the corner of your mouth. And in a little more than a week now—I shall!

Lorena Hickok to Eleanor Roosevelt
(Faber, 1980, p. 152)

Anna Eleanor Roosevelt (October 11, 1884-November 7, 1962), American social reformer, humanitarian, first lady. Eleanor was born into an old colonial New England family of affluence and notoriety. Their politics had been anti-Semitic, anti-Negro, anti-women's suffrage, and less than compassionate to the poor. Eleanor was not favored by her parents, who died when she was ten. She was considered an ugly and gloomy child, learning early on the hardships of being an outsider. Eleanor dedicated her long life to championing the struggles of the underdog, and is considered by many historians to be the most important American woman of the twentieth century.

ER and Hick on the run

Eleanor Roosevelt married her cousin, Franklin D. Roosevelt (March 17, 1905), who later became governor of New York and then president of the United States. Eleanor, a tireless crusader for human rights who often dictated 100 letters a day, wrestled with civil rights issues for black Americans, coal miners, women, child laborers, and the hungry and impoverished; she was U.S. ambassador to the United Nations; and she worked with the National Association for the Advancement of Colored People (NAACP) to end discrimination against blacks by the military. When America was sending boatloads of Jewish refugees back to their deaths in Nazi Germany, Eleanor set up a detention camp for Jewish refugees in Oswego, New York. She also was responsible for the Universal Declaration of Human Rights adopted by the United Nations General Assembly (December 10, 1948). Her contributions to humanity are too numerous and vast for the scope of this biography. Eleanor resigned from the Daughters of the American Revolution (DAR) when they refused to allow African-American opera singer Marian Anderson to sing at Constitution Hall (1939). Roosevelt instead arranged for Anderson's concert to be on

Eleanor Roosevelt   Lorena Hickok

the steps of the Lincoln Memorial, attended by 75,000; Eleanor listened to it from a terrace at the White House.

Lorena Alice Hickok (March 7, 1893-May 1, 1968), American journalist. As a child, Lorena was battered by her father, and her mother died when she was thirteen. Hick, as she was known most of her life, was overweight. She was a journalist from 1913 to 1932, working for many different newspapers and periodicals, covering a variety of subjects from homemaking to Democratic Party politics. She traveled the country sending reports of her observations on the successes and failures of the New Deal to the Federal Emergency Relief Administration. The Associated Press assigned Hick to cover First Lady Eleanor Roosevelt (1932). Eleanor and Hick traveled together extensively and became fast friends.

When Eleanor discovered that her husband was having an affair (1918) with her social secretary, Lucy Mercer, she asked for a divorce. Franklin's domineering mother would have none of this scandal in the family, and the divorce was refused. Eleanor moved in with two female friends and reevaluated her life in family and politics.

FDR with another mistress, Missy Lehand (center), and ER

Mercer (April 26, 1891-July 31, 1948) lived at the White House as the president's mistress, and Hickok lived at the White House (1940-1944) as Eleanor's lover and companion. More than 3,000 letters are extant from Eleanor to Hick, many of them juicy with intimate details professing their requited love. Hick wrote biographies of Eleanor and Helen Keller. Hick and Eleanor co-authored *Ladies of Courage* (1954).

Eleanor is buried with her husband. Hickok's ashes were scattered.

BIBLIOGRAPHY

Cook, Blanche Wiesen (1992). *Eleanor Roosevelt.* New York: Penguin Books.
Faber, Doris (1980). *The Life of Lorena Hickok: E. R.'s friend.* New York: William Morrow and Company.

CHARLOTTE CUSHMAN AND EMMA STEBBINS
AND EDMONIA LEWIS

Charlotte Saunders Cushman (July 23, 1816-February 18, 1876), American actress. Cushman's legendary life of celebrity began in poverty and child labor. Considered a serious person at times, Cushman's theatrical success on the American East Coast was well-earned but sporadic. When she arrived in London, Cushman was hailed as a shining star and thence recognized internationally. She played *Romeo* to her sister's *Juliet* (1845), and in her career played thirty roles impersonating men. She performed for Queen Victoria (1848), and toured the United States (1849-1852). Cushman had made her fortune early and semi-retired (1852) at thirty-six to her home in London, wintering in Rome. Following an emotional farewell performance (November 7, 1874), 25,000 people gathered in front of Cushman's New York Hotel to give her a roaring ovation. Charlotte Cushman was elected into New York University's Hall of Fame (1915).

In Rome (1857) Cushman met Emma Stebbins (September 1, 1815-October 24, 1882), American sculptor, painter. Stebbins' career as an artist began with crayons, watercolors, and oils: her first major

Charlotte Cushman   Emma Stebbins

exhibit was at the National Academy (1855). In Rome she soon shifted her medium to sculpture, making a bust of Cushman (1859-1960). Her bronze statue of Horace Mann was installed in front of the State House in Boston (1865), and her famous *Angel of the Waters* was commissioned for the Bethesda Fountain in Central Park, New York City (May 1873). Stebbins and Cushman returned permanently to America in 1870. They were lovers for nineteen years. Stebbins compiled *Charlotte Cushman: Her Letters and Memories of Her Life* (1878).

Also in Rome, Cushman and Stebbins met Edmonia Lewis (née Wildfire Lewis, c. July 4, 1845-c. 1911), American sculptor. Lewis is an exotic heroine in the landscape of American heritage. Her African-American father and her Chippewa mother both died before she was five. Wildfire was raised by her mother's sister among the Chippewa. She attended Oberlin College (1859), financed by her Californian gold miner brother, Sunrise. This is quite an accomplishment in itself, considering most women did not go to college, certainly very few women of color, and even fewer biracial women. At Oberlin she changed her name to Edmonia. The college still owns her sculpture, *The Muse, Urania*.

Lewis's first work was a medallion of the head of abolitionist martyr John Brown, which was advertised in William Lloyd Garrison's *Liberator* (1864). Later that year, Lewis's fame was established with her bust of Colonel Robert Gould Shaw, the Bostonian who led America's first all-black regiment in the Union Army. One hundred copies were made of this bust (1865); this garnered Lewis enough money to travel to Europe, where she settled in Rome. She was visited in her studio near the Spanish Steps by Pope Pius IX, who gave a papal blessing to her work. Her sculpture caused a minor uproar at the Centennial Exposition of 1876 in Philadelphia. Her marble bust of

Edmonia Lewis

Henry Wadsworth Longfellow is at Harvard College's Schlesinger Library, and three other sculptures are at the San Jose Library.

Lewis is alleged to have been the part-time lover of Charlotte Cushman by some lesbian herstorians. They were at least friends and comrades in a large community of lesbian American artists living in Rome that included the famous bisexual actress Fanny Kemble. Lewis's death and whereabouts are unknown.

KAREN THOMPSON AND SHARON KOWALSKI AND PATRICIA BRESSER

Sharon Kowalski (August 8, 1956–), American motorcyclist, free spirit. Kowalski was in a serious automobile accident in November 1983. Her car was struck by a drunk driver, killing her four-year-old niece, and leaving Kowalski in a coma. Karen Thompson (July 24, 1947–), American educator, had been her lover for four years.

A Minnesota judge denied Thompson the right to visit her adult lover (July 23, 1985), and gave custodial rights of Kowalski to her

Patricia Bresser, Sharon Kowalski, and Karen Thompson

homophobic Catholic parents. But this did not deter Thompson. "Some people would rather view Sharon as a vegetable than as a lesbian," Thompson said. She then marshaled support from lesbians, feminists, people with disabilities, gay men, and organizations (including the National Organization for Women) from around the country. In August 1988, there were protest rallies in twenty-one American cities, testament to Thompson's heroic lesbian American courage. After three-and-a-half years barring visitation, on February 2, 1989, Thompson won a court victory, and a victory for all queer bonders in America, to custodial rights and the ability to care for her lover, Sharon Kowalski, who remains quadriplegic.

In our last phone conversation, Thompson cautiously "came out" to me and spoke of their polyamorous household of three. Lovingly joining this legendary lesbian American couple, in an overlapping relationship, is Patricia Bresser (August 23, 1955–), American nurse. Twenty-three years after her accident, Sharon Kowalski has just recently recovered some motor coordination, and has begun to talk again.

I told Thompson that now I'd have to move her marriage from Peer Love to a different chapter of the book, Overlapping Love. I think it was reassuring to her to know that there is a place in queer love for polyamorous people. Before we hung up, Thompson told me, "Our love continues to grow daily."

BIBLIOGRAPHY

Thompson, Karen, personal communications: November 1, 1994; April 23, 2007. Reprinted by permission.

Chapter 4

Pattern of Interclass Love

And now I'll strum a lyre that's gay
And sing of boys with whom the gods did play.

Ovid, *Metamorphoses*

Interclass love is a relationship between two (or more) same-gender persons from differing socioeconomic classes.

AIDI AND DONG XIAN

Aidi (–1 BCE), Chinese emperor. Aidi, the last emperor of the Former Han Dynasty, had many male lovers. But the most legendary was Dong Xian. As the two men lay napping together, Dong resting his head on Aidi's large sleeve, the emperor was called away to attend to courtly matters. Rather than awaken his drowsy lover, Aidi cut off his sleeve. Homosexual courtiers soon began the fashion of cutting their sleeves. In Chinese culture and literature, male homosexual love is referred to as *duanxiu,* meaning "the cut sleeve." Aidi had no sons, bequeathing his title to Dong.

BIBLIOGRAPHY

Hinsch, Bret (1992). *Passions of the Cut Sleeve: The Male Homosexual Tradition in China.* University of California Press.

RICHARD THE LIONHEART AND BLONDEL

Richard I (September 8, 1157-April 6, 1199), English king. Richard I was an accomplished warrior well known for his chivalrous manner. He married Berengaria of Navarre; they had no children. Richard the Lionheart spent only six to ten months of his eleven-year reign (1189-1199) in England. The rest of the time he was off warring. Richard the Lionheart joined the Third Crusade to the Holy Land (1190) in an attempt to expel Moslem control from Jerusalem. Instead, he struck an equal-access agreement with their leader, Saladin.

Upon returning from Palestine, Richard I was captured in Austria and imprisoned by Leopold V (1192). Legend has it that the king was located by his lover, Blondel de Nesle, French troubadour. Blondel roamed the countryside singing the first lines of a love song that he and King Richard had written together. When Richard sang back from his cell, Blondel alerted the English army as to their king's whereabouts.

No evidence whatever & the evidence for RI's homosexuality is absolute junk

CHRISTINA AND EBBA SPARRE

Christina (December 8, 1626-April 19, 1689), Queen of Sweden. When Christina was born to King Gustavus (II) Adolphus and Maria Eleonora of Brandenburg, the midwives announced a baby boy. This may have been due to her parents imperiously wanting a male successor, and/or due to the speculation that Christina was intersex (a her-

maphrodite). Christina was irrefutably gender-variant, cross-dressing by her mid-teens. Of Queen Christina, Father Marmerschied, priest to the Spanish Ambassador, said, "There is nothing feminine about her except her sex. Her voice, her manner of speaking, her walk, her style, her ways are all quite masculine" (Goldsmith, 1933, p. 75).

King Gustavus died when Christina was six, and her queenly duties were performed by a regency until she turned eighteen (1644) and was crowned "King of Sweden." Christina

Queen Christina of Sweden   was a queer child who grew into a queer adult, her personal orientation often at odds with the environment. It is reported that she suffered the wrath of her parents wishing she were a boy. Christina was given an exemplary education, as well as lessons in fencing, riding, shooting, and military tactics. She spoke eight languages. She was groomed a monarch to rule. But Christina didn't like politics and preferred instead discussions of science and philosophy with artists and scholars, notably Descartes. Queen Christina refused to marry and produce an heir for the throne. She lavished her friends with titles and money, giving away half of the crown lands. Christina associated mostly with men, letting go of the ladies-in-waiting routine. But there was one particularly romantic relationship she'd had since her teens. Queen Christina did not hide her affectionate bond, referring to her lover as her "bedfellow."

Ebba Sparre (dates unknown, nationality unknown), countess, bedfellow. Queen Christina wrote to Sparre, *la belle comtesse:*

> and if you remember the power you have over me, you will also remember I have been in possession of your love for twelve years; I belong to you so utterly, that it will never be possible for you to lose me; and only, when I die, shall I cease loving you. (Goldsmith, 1933, p. 70)

Too queer for queendom, Christina abdicated her throne (1654) to her cousin, Karl-Gustav (Charles X). She wandered Europe cross-dressed, a person without a country, and converted to Catholicism. At her cousin's death (1660), Christina returned to Sweden to reclaim her throne but was unable to succeed. She returned (1667) in another attempt to regain rule, but was denied permission to enter Stockholm because of her conversion from Lutheran to Catholicism.

Christina settled in Rome where, at 60, she met Italian opera singer Angelica Georgini. Christina patronized women in the arts, notably the introduction of female opera singers as replacement for male *castrati*. Georgini enjoyed the sponsorship and romantic interest of the queen of queer. Christina died in Rome and is buried in St. Peter's Basilica.

BIBLIOGRAPHY

Goldsmith, Margaret (1933). *Christina of Sweden: A Psychological Biography.* New York: Doubleday, Doran & Co., Inc.

COLETTE AND MISSY

Sidonie Gabrielle Colette (January 28, 1873-August 3, 1954), French writer, actor. Colette wrote novels, short stories, plays, memoirs and more. Most notable were her *Claudine* and *Chéri* series. Many of her literary contributions are stories of women seeking independent lives, often as lovers with other women.

Colette was bisexual and had three marriages. Her first (1893-1910), at age nineteen, was to thirty-five-year-old Henri Gauthier-Villars. He was reported to have locked her in her room until she finished writing her daily quotient. He is responsible for starting her on her career as a writer, but he kept all of her royalties. Colette's second marriage (1912-1923) was to Baron Henri de Jouvenel. He married her two months after impregnating her with her only child, a daughter. They were divorced when de Jouvenel discovered Colette having an affair with his son. Her third marriage (1935) to Maurice Goudeket lasted until her death.

Colette also had many affairs with women, notably actress and writer Renée Vivien and French film star Marguerite Moreno. But perhaps her most celebrated *amitié amoureuse* was that with Marquise de Belbœuf (née Mathilde de Morny, 1862-1944), French aristocrat. "Missy"—as she was known—was the youngest daughter of the Duc de Morny, niece of Napoleon III, and great-granddaughter of Empress Josephine. Missy's mother was Russian Princess Sophie Troubetzkoi. As a tomboy daughter, Missy was considered an ugly embarrassment; this may have encouraged her to develop as a unique individual. Missy always kept her hair short, was out about her lesbianism, always cross-dressed—dinner jackets in the evening, overalls as she tinkered with mechanics in the day—and in public was often mistaken for a man. She was married for a short time to the Marquis de Belbœuf.

Colette and Missy met in 1906 and their affair lasted into the early 1920s. They remained friends for life. Missy wrote a mime play, *Rêve d'Égypte* (1907), in which she and Colette co-starred at the Moulin-Rouge. Missy played the role of a male archaeologist of Egyptology who falls in love with a mummy. The mummy (Colette) begins unwrapping her bandages and proceeds into a near-nude wild sensual dance that culminates in a long passionate kiss with the scholar (Missy). This rebirthing/coming-out theater piece proved too much for the audience who threw pillows, footstools, matchboxes, and orange peelings at the stage.

Colette wore an ankle bracelet that was engraved "I belong to Missy." Of historical interest, in Paris, Colette and Missy applied for, but were denied, a marriage license (1907).

Of her numerous awards, Colette received the Legion of Honor: chevalier (1920), officer (1928), commander (1936), and grand officer (1953). As she was dying, the Catholic Church refused her request of last rites. Colette was the first woman granted a state funeral, France's highest posthumous honor. She is buried at Père Lachaise. Missy committed suicide hara-kiri style.

BIBLIOGRAPHY

Crosland, Margaret (1973). *Colette: The Difficulty of Loving*. New York: Dell Publishing Co.

Mitchell, Yvonne (1975). *Colette: A Taste for Life*. New York: Harcourt Brace Javonovich.

FREDERICK THE GREAT AND HANS VON KATTE

Frederick II (January 24, 1712-August 17, 1786), Prussian king. Little Frederick was a small, sensitive, and effeminate boy who was intellectually stimulated by the French arts and literature. His bombastic and tyrannical father, Frederick William I was anti-intellectual, homophobic, and a brutal ruler. Little Frederick was beaten and verbally abused by his father almost every day of his childhood.

At age eighteen, Frederick fell in love with twenty-six-year-old Lieutenant Hans Hermann von Katte (c.1704-1730), Prussian military officer. Von Katte has been described as well-educated, an extremely handsome freethinker, and a lover of the arts. To avoid the wrath of the king, Frederick and Hans ran away together (eloped), but were apprehended and returned. The king overturned the court's sentencing of von Katte to life imprisonment, and instead ordered him beheaded. He also ordered his son to witness the execution of his lover. At the moment of beheading, Frederick passed out and then hallucinated for a day and a half.

Frederick the Great was an atheist who ascended the throne (1740) and ruled Prussia with a strong and handsome military, greatly expanding sponsorship of the arts. He enacted the abolition of torture, granted pardons for sodomites, and increased religious tolerance. After his unwanted arranged marriage to Elizabeth Christine of Brunswick-Bevern, they immediately separated. Frederick had no children and no female friends or companions. His courtiers were all male and reportedly of a visually appealing nature. Frederick the Great's brother Henry was also homosexual. Frederick is buried at the Church of Peace in Sanssouci Park.

LEOPOLDINA AND MARIA GRAHAM

Maria Leopoldina (c. 1797-December 11, 1826), Austrian-Brazilian empress. Leopoldina, sister of Marie Louise (Napoleon's second wife), married Brazilian emperor Pedro, brother to Portugal's King John. This was an unhappy arranged marriage. Leopoldina was well-educated and horrified at the lack of culture in the New World colony. Her uneducated husband was a king who preferred the company of stable grooms.

Maria Graham (1785-November 28, 1842), English governess, writer. Maria married naval captain Thomas Graham in India, and in 1821 they immigrated to Rio de Janeiro. Thomas died soon thereafter on a passage to Chile around Cape Horn.

The widow Graham, an educated woman, found herself in dire straits. She applied to the benevolence of Empress Leopoldina. The empress fell in love with Graham. She gave Graham an apartment in the palace and a job as governess. Their intergenerational and interclass love soon became annoying to Pedro. The women spent all of their time together reading and discussing art. The entire court became jealous of their shared affection. Graham eventually returned to England and married English painter Augustus Callcott.

Real historians tell a very different story

EDWARD II AND PIERS GAVESTON

Edward II (April 25, 1284-September 21, 1327), English king, prince of Wales. Despite his excellent military training and record, Edward despised warfare and competition. He preferred thatching roofs, digging ditches, gambling, and carousing with common folk. Brought into court (1300) as a companion to Edward was an orphaned son of a French knight, Piers Gaveston (c. 1282-June 1312). Edward admired Piers' ribald manner, and the two became inseparable and unabashed lovers.

King Edward I banished his son's lover from England in 1307, but Edward II ascended the throne the same year, bringing Piers back home to their interclass relationship. Edward honored his father's arrangements and married (1308) Princess Isabella of France. They had four children. But Isabella was jealous of Gaveston, as Edward publicly showered his affections on him and not her. Edward made Gaveston Earl of Cornwall and Regent of Ireland. Isabella plotted with the barons and power elite, returned to France and garnered support, and had Piers Gaveston beheaded.

Edward II and Piers Gaveston

Edward II had a new lover (c. 1320), Hugh le Despenser the younger, whom Isabella disliked equally. It is chronicled that Isabella (aka "the She-Wolf of France") ordered the execution of Hugh; she said he should have his genitals cut off and burned before him, and then be beheaded. Isabella, with her lover Roger de Mortimer, continued to plot against her husband and eventually forced Edward to abdicate the throne. King Edward II was then imprisoned and subjected to various humiliations before being murdered by guards who allegedly rammed a red-hot iron poker up his rectum.

MARQUIS DE SADE AND LATOUR

Perhaps the most misunderstood man in human history, whose mere name sends shudders of troubled shadow through our collective psyche, is Donatien Alphonse François, comte de Sade (June 2, 1740-December 2, 1814), French writer, libertine, iconoclast.

De Sade's voluminous literary works—half of which were destroyed by his older son—are licentious, pansexually explicit, and bombastically anti-Catholic, notably *Justine, or The Misfortunes of Virtue* (1787/published in 1791) and its sister novel, *Juliette, or The Prosperity of Vice* (c. 1797). His legend has been inextricably linked to and confused with his fiction. Much of his lascivious stories are physically impossible—black humor that many citizens failed to understand. De Sade's written works are often censored by governments and religious institutions. Where these works do exist they are oftentimes kept locked and bound, as de Sade probably would have liked, in hidden secret subterranean corridors of danger and darkness. De Sade's philosophies on nature and society and his observations on human sexuality and behavior have influenced and enlightened many latter scientists, notably psychotherapists Sigmund Freud and Carl Jung. His *120 Days of Sodom* (1785), microscopically written on both sides of a single roll of paper, 5 inches by 15 yards, was discovered 100 years later under the floorboards of the Bastille; de Sade had hidden the manuscript there while he was a prisoner. De Sade spent almost thirty years behind bars.

His first major public sex scandal was when Rose Keller, a part-time prostitute hired by de Sade, brought him to court for beating her mercilessly—it is alleged as an attempt to extort money from de Sade. The courts, however, were most incensed by the fact that this promiscuity occurred on Easter Sunday.

A marriage was arranged on May 17, 1763, between the impoverished but landed and entitled Marquis de Sade and the wealthy but title-less bourgeois Renée-Pélagie de Montreuil. En route to their honeymoon, de Sade ordered the coachman to pull over when they came upon a field of wild white lilies. Smiling at his bride, he poured bottles of red wine onto the pure blossoms. De Sade challenged public standards in his dramatic style and double-entendre. De Sade openly had an affair with his wife's sister as he did with many other women. Renée-Pélagie loved her husband and mostly stood by him despite his outrageous behavior and the scorn she consequently suffered.

It was de Sade's mother-in-law who continually petitioned the courts (after her access to Versailles) to lock up her scandalous and embarrassing son-in-law. But it was de Sade's trial in absentia (1772) at Marseilles that turned fate against him forever. Of all the "crimes against nature" of which de Sade was found guilty, this most serious allegation of sodomy brought the sentence of death. He was to be executed with his lover, Latour (dates unknown), French valet. During this period of de Sade's long life, his primary companion, sex partner, and lover was Latour. Although de Sade was pansexual and engaged in a variety of sexual interactions, he was primarily heterosexual. However, his favorite adventure was to be sodomized by well-endowed Latour, while de Sade flagellated the plump bottoms of female hookers. During one similar scene where Latour was sodomizing de Sade while de Sade sodomized a hooker, de Sade referred to his valet Latour as "Monsieur le Marquis," and then Latour referred to de Sade as "Lefleur."

Latour was possibly an illegitimate son of a nobleman whom de Sade befriended. He was tall with long hair and was known to wear blue-and-yellow-striped sailor's outfits. De Sade would send Latour to procure sex partners and stage their erotic scenes. Latour was responsible for later helping de Sade escape from prison. With his death sentence for buggering the boss hanging over his condemned-to-be-strangled head, Latour vanished (1777). It is said that he was last seen boarding a ship. For the New World? I like to dream that Latour came to America and pollinated this land.

De Sade commanded the storming of the Bastille through a tin pipe from inside his cell. His longtime campaign advocating egalitarianism and the wanton laws of nature as more ideal than the tyranny of Church and aristocracy worked both in his favor and to his demise. He is one of the few aristocrats who did not lose his head during the bloody Revolution and the following Reign of Terror. He was made a judge by Napoleon, but was dismissed for his lack of guilty verdicts, including his mother-in-law, whom he exonerated under the condition she exile herself from France. He further compromised his standing with the new elite by parroting Napoleon and Josephine's sexualities in his book *Philosophy in the Bedroom* (1795). De Sade's final intimate relationship was with actress Marie-Constance Quesnet, who was half his age and remained his faithful mistress for his last pain-filled twenty-four years. De Sade died in the mental asylum at Charenton, where he was buried. His skeleton was later exhumed for scientific study and then it disappeared.

De Sade wanted more than anything to be a playwright, but had terrible misfortune and disappointment in this career. Perhaps his greatest success at being a playwright was in his final obese years at Charenton. There he directed the insane in shadow productions of humanity.

BIBLIOGRAPHY

de Beauvoir, Simone (1953). *Must We Burn de Sade?* New York: Grove Press.

Hayman, Ronald (1978). *De Sade: A Critical Biography.* New York: Thomas Y. Crowell, Publishers.

Thomas, Donald (1992). *The Marquis de Sade: A New Biography.* New Jersey: Citadel Press.

AMY LOWELL AND ADA RUSSELL

I put your leaves aside,
One by one:
The stiff broad outer leaves;
The smaller ones,
Pleasant to touch, veined with purple;
The glazed inner leaves,
Until you stood up like a white flower
Swaying slightly in the evening wind.

Amy Lowell
(Lowell, 1955, p. 211)

Amy Lawrence Lowell (February 9, 1874-May 12, 1925), American poet. Lowell's life changed forever at age thirty-eight, when she published her first book of Imagist poetry and consummated her love with Ada Dwyer Russell (1863-1952), American actress, divorcée and mother, editor.

Amy Lowell, c. 1916   Ada Russell, c. 1916

They met (1909) while Russell was touring New England to promote *Dawn of a Tomorrow*. But it wasn't until 1912 when Russell was starring in *The Deep Purple* that Lowell seduced her into forming an intergenerational and interclass alliance at Lowell's mansion (Sevenals, in Brookline, Massachusetts), which lasted until Lowell's death.

Of Lowell's dozen books of poetry, a two-volume biography of John Keats, and many essays, it was her poetry collection *What's O'Clock* (1925) that won her a posthumous Pulitzer Prize (1926). Much of Lowell's poetry spoke of love, mostly for Russell. The forty-three poems in the "Two Speak Together" section of *Pictures of the Floating World* (1919) are perhaps the most complete and beautiful record of their love.

Lowell was a mere five feet tall and obese (250 pounds) most of her life. Unconfirmed reports say she was butch-acting and femme-dressing. She certainly had her own brand of gender variance. Lowell addressed Russell as "Peter." In a time when it was considered ill-mannered for women to smoke, Lowell regularly indulged in small black Manila cigars. It is reported that she once caused a man to blush by comparing her unwrapping of a cigar to the undressing, layer by layer, of a lady; she then lit the cigar and inhaled seductively.

It remains irrefutable that the dramatic entrance and devoted companionship of Ada Russell into Amy Lowell's privileged and sybaritic life is what caused the poet to finally blossom. Lowell's ashes were interred without religious services in Mount Auburn Cemetery, Cambridge. She left her entire fortune to Ada.

BIBLIOGRAPHY

Faderman, Lillian, "Cigar-Smoking Sappho." *The Advocate,* February 13, 1990.
Kelly, Katie, "Amy Was a Right-on Woman," *Village Voice*, January 12, 1976.
Lowell, Amy (1955). *The Complete Poetical Works of Amy Lowell.* Boston: Houghton Mifflin Co.

ROCK HUDSON AND MARC CHRISTIAN

Rock Hudson (né Roy Harold Scherer Jr., November 17, 1925-October 2, 1985), American movie star. Hudson starred in several dozen films, notably *Giant* (1956) and *Pillow Talk* (1959), and in the television series *McMillan and Wife* (1970s). Hudson entered his career trading on his good looks and capped teeth. In his first film, *Fighter Squadron* (1948), it took thirty-eight takes for Hudson to successfully complete one line.

Hudson's active libido reportedly led him into countless homosexual interactions with friends, tricks, and hustlers. One of Rock's friends for thirty-five years was actor George Nader, whose companion, Mark Miller, became Rock's manager. When a magazine threatened to expose America's manly symbol of sexual virility as a homosexual, Hudson married (possibly bisexual) actress Phyllis Gates (1955-1958). She divorced him on grounds of "mental cruelty."

Hudson, fifty-six, met his intergenerational lover, twenty-nine-year-old Marc Christian, (c. 1953–), American musicologist, in 1982. He hired Christian to convert his large collection of 78s onto tape. Christian moved into Hudson's estate in April 1983.

It was publicly confirmed by Hudson's French doctors that he had AIDS (1985). Hudson did not voluntarily admit this information. Christian encountered the news of his lover's illness via television. Hudson knew that he had AIDS but never told Christian about it, engaging in unprotected anal sex with him dozens of times.

Upon his death, Hudson's estate was estimated at $14 million. He left nothing to Christian, who sued the estate for $10 million and offered to settle. But Miller and others lambasted Christian via the media, calling him a "gold digger" and a "hustler." After an increase in the punitive damages, the jury awarded Christian more than $21 million (February, 1989). The judge diminished the award to $5.5 million.

Even after his forced disclosure of having AIDS, Rock Hudson never publicly admitted that he was gay. It is believed that he never donated a penny to any gay organization or cause. In 1985, it was reported that Hudson gifted $250,000 to the American Foundation for AIDS Research. But this money was not a gift; it was a loan for seed money, and was paid back to Hudson's estate. Returning on his last flight from Paris to Los Angeles, Hudson chartered a 747 at the cost of $300,000.

BIBLIOGRAPHY

Askori, Emilia, "Rock's Pillow Talk Didn't Mention AIDS." *Los Angeles Herald Examiner,* Januray 12, 1989.

Feldman, Paul and Tobar, Hector, "Jury Raises Award to Hudson's Lover by $7.25 Million." *Los Angeles Times,* February 18, 1989.

Rosenberg, Howard, "Inner Man Stays in the Closet in Rock Hudson." *Los Angeles Times,* January 8, 1990.

FREDDIE MERCURY AND JIM HUTTON

Freddie Mercury (né Farrokh Bulsara, September 5, 1946-November 24, 1991), African-British rock star. In his celebrated career as lead singer for the British rock group Queen, Mercury attained international fame and amassed a fortune. In 1983 Mercury met and began courting Jim Hutton (January 4, 1949–), Irish-British barber, gardener, companion. After a tumultuous beginning, these two lovers committed to each other and to a frenzied world-class romance of fast jets and packed stadiums. Mercury wore a wedding ring given to him by Hutton, and referred to Hutton as his husband. In the arms of his lover, Freddie Mercury died of AIDS.

Jim Hutton and Freddie Mercury in Munich, 1985

BIBLIOGRAPHY

Hutton, Jim (1994). *Mercury and Me*. London: Bloomsbury.

Chapter 5

Pattern of Interethnic Love

We are never so defenseless against suffering as when we love.

Sigmund Freud
(Fisher, 1992, p. 162)

Interethnic love is a relationship between two (or more) same-gender persons of different ethnicities. Queer couples have a noticeably juicy frequency of interethnic love.

Xenophilia is the erotic love of foreigners and strangers, of people of a different skin color, nationality, or tribe. Xenophilia can be a sexual arousal to foreign languages, accents, or to mannerisms or customs from another culture. Some individuals' xenophilia is fueled by their societal taboo, what sexologist Jack Morin refers to as "the naughtiness factor."

Many people enthusiastically engage in the discussion of "Why are some people gay? Is it nature, is it nurture?" But the question of greater sexological interest would be, "What makes most people straight?"

In his theory on the origins of heterosexuality, Daryl Bem suggests that heterosexuals are attracted to one another because in most societies gender segregation is the norm, creating obstacles to—and a mythos of—the opposite gender. His theory is known as "Exotic Becomes Erotic." It is my belief that Bem's theory could account for the high rate of xenophilia in persons who seek same-gender affection.

A common thread is found in examples of interethnic love: a raw theme of passion and strife. Each of the following lovers struggled politically, socially, sexually, as well as romantically. Driven by a sense of duty and righteousness, most of them suffered greatly. They all wanted the world to be a better place, and so made heroic efforts to accomplish this noble goal.

Legacies of Love: A Heritage of Queer Bonding
© 2008 by The Haworth Press, Taylor & Francis Group. All rights reserved.
doi:10.1300/5890_06

LAWRENCE OF ARABIA AND AHMED DAHOUM

I loved you, so I drew these tides of men into my hands
and wrote my will across the sky in stars
To gain you Freedom, the seven-pillared worthy house,
that your eyes might be shining for me
When we came.

Lawrence of Arabia
Seven Pillars of Wisdom

Thomas Edward Lawrence, aka Lawrence of Arabia (August 16, 1888-May 19, 1935), British warrior, explorer, scholar, writer. Lawrence of Arabia's life was a struggle between the political and the private. His archaeological studies at Oxford led him to Syria and Meso-

Lawrence of Arabia, c. 1912   Ahmed Dahoum, c. 1912

potamia (1911), where he learned colloquial Arabic. He served with the British intelligence in Egypt during World War I, and afterward joined the Arabs in combat against Turkish oppression (1916). He wrote accounts of his being captured and imprisoned by the Turks, and their subsequent gang rape of him before he escaped, in his memoir *Seven Pillars of Wisdom* (1926). His heroic celebrity forever dissolved his anonymity. Lawrence joined the Royal Air Force (RAF) under a pseudonym, and assumed pen names. It is during his stint with the RAF that *The New York Times* reported Lawrence employed a fellow officer ". . . to administer regular flagellation on his bare buttocks, for sexual excitement."

Ahmed Dahoum (né Selim Ahmed, c. 1897-1916), Syrian warrior, photographer, aide. Dahoum was fifteen when he met Lawrence, twenty-three, the latter suffering from near-fatal dysentery. Dahoum nursed Lawrence back to health, Lawrence forever referring to him as "Sheik Ahmed." Heterosexual biographers fumblingly insist that this intergenerational and interethnic relationship was nonsexual, and that Lawrence remained celibate his entire life. The Arabs of the communities where Lawrence and Dahoum lived professed to the contrary that their relationship was homosexual. They did not "come out," and neither did they hide their great affection for each other.

Lawrence took Sheik Ahmed back to England, ostensibly to give him a Western education. Lawrence carved well-endowed gargoyles modeled after Dahoum, causing quite a controversy. Biographers insist that Dahoum could not possibly have reduced himself to modeling in the nude. Lawrence was fond of uniforms and motorcycles. Recent journal discoveries and witness testimony place Lawrence as a frequenter of gay establishments, a member of a leather fraternity, and as an accomplished S-M bottom.

Dahoum died in a typhoid epidemic. Lawrence died of complications from brain damage due to a motorcycle accident. His funeral was at St. Nicholas's Church in Moreton.

BIBLIOGRAPHY

Trevor-Roper, Hugh, "A Humbug Exalted." *The New York Times,* November 6, 1977.

Wilson, Jeremy (1989). *Lawrence of Arabia.* New York: Atheneum.

JAMES BALDWIN
AND LUCIEN HAPPERSBERGER

I starved in Paris for a while, but I learned something. For one thing I fell in love. Or, more accurately, I realized, and accepted for the first time that love was not merely a general human possibility, nor merely the disaster it had so often, by then, been for me—according to me—nor was it something that happened to other people, like death, nor was it merely a mortal danger: it was among *my* possibilities, for here it was, breathing and belching beside me, and it was the key to life.

James Baldwin
upon meeting Lucien Happersberger
(Kenan, 1994, pp. 71-72)

James Arthur Baldwin (August 2, 1924-December 1, 1987), American writer, human rights activist. Baldwin heroically surfed the margins of his life. As a child he obsessively read *Uncle Tom's Cabin*—his mother having to hide it from him—because, it is reported, he identified with the goodness and loyalty of Uncle Tom. But inquiring queer minds may wonder if perhaps there was also an identification with the effeminate mulatto slave, Adolph, possibly the first representation in American literature of an American queer male of color.

James Baldwin

Baldwin wove his life out of goodness and loyalty, out of being black and being gay, out of being a wanderer and having a home, out of questing for an elusive love. He was a poet, playwright, essayist, and the author of more than a dozen books, most notably, *Notes of a Native Son* (1955), *Giovanni's Room* (1956), and *The Fire Next Time* (1963). His tireless dedication to championing civil rights is legendary. Baldwin spent much of his adult life in France, and in 1986 was awarded by President Mitterand the most prestigious Commander of the Legion of Honor.

On his first trip to Paris, Baldwin in 1949 met the man he would spend his life being obsessed with: Lucien Happersberger (1932-?), Swiss heartthrob. Happersberger was a seventeen-year-old runaway looking for adventure in Paris, the City of Light. The avant-garde black-American writer was an exotic catch for the sheltered white boy. Baldwin fell fast for Happersberger, and they shared their *sous* and life and love. When Baldwin took ill from their debauched city life (1951), Lucien took him home to recover at his family's Alpine chalet in Loèche-les-Bains, Switzerland. None of the 600 villagers had ever seen a black person before.

In 1952, Happersberger married. This left James devastated, even though he was later named godfather to the resulting children. Happersberger visited Baldwin in America (1955), and remained a loyal friend for life, but not as romantically as Baldwin longed for. Happersberger moved to New York (1964) to manage Baldwin's budding career as a playwright, helping with the Broadway production of *Blues for Mr. Charlie*. Happersberger fell in love with and married the leading black-American actress, Diana Sands. Once again Baldwin suffered losing his Lucien. It appears as though Happersberger's youthful exploration of homosexual love with Baldwin was but a phase in the development of his predominantly interethnic heterosexual identity.

James Baldwin died of cancer at his farmhouse in Saint-Paul-de-Vence, France, with Happersberger at his side. A week later at his funeral at the Cathedral of St. John the Divine, New York City, 5,000 mourners paid their respects to one of America's greatest literary voices.

BIBLIOGRAPHY

Kenan, Randall (1994). *James Baldwin.* New York: Chelsea House Publishers.
Stowe, Harriet Beecher (1852/1938). *Uncle Tom's Cabin,* or, *Life Among the Lowly.* New York: The Heritage Press.

SYLVIA BEACH AND ADRIENNE MONNIER

Sylvia Beach and Adrienne Monnier at Shakespeare and Co.

Sylvia Woodbridge Beach (March 14, 1887-October 5, 1962), American bookseller, publisher. Adrienne Monnier (April 26, 1892-June 19, 1955), French bookseller, publisher. Beach and Monnier met in Paris around 1917, and were lovers for more than thirty-five years. Monnier was the proprietress of La Maison des Amis des Livres, established in 1915 and considered by many to be the elite avant-garde bookstore of Paris. She encouraged Beach to open a similar bookstore with English and American titles to meet the needs of the growing expatriate community. Beach's Shakespeare and Company, established in 1919, was across the rue de l'Odéon from Monnier's bookshop. Together they merged the literati of the French and American worlds of letters. Beach was the benefactor of writer James Joyce and was instrumental in getting his works published.

Monnier was more comfortable in the country, and every summer she and Beach vacationed in Savoy. Beach was granted the prestigious Legion of Honor (1938), but was forced to close Shakespeare and Company (1941) due to Nazi harassment. She was later arrested and interned at Vittel for six months until the Allied liberation. Sylvia Beach died of a heart attack, and was buried at the Princeton Cemetery. Adrienne Monnier died of a fatal dose of sleeping pills after suffering from an incurable and debilitating illness.

Monnier and Beach

BIBLIOGRAPHY

Fitch, Noel Riley (1985). *Sylvia Beach and the Lost Generation.* New York: W. W. Norton & Co.
McDougall, Richard (1976). *The Very Rich Hours of Adrienne Monnier.* New York: Scribner's.

PATRICK WHITE
AND MANOLY LASCARIS

Patrick Victor Martindale White (May 28, 1912-September 30, 1990), British-Australian novelist and playwright, gentleman farmer. White authored dozens of literary works, most notably *Voss* (1957) and *The Twyborn Affair* (1979). Among White's many distinguished awards is the Nobel Prize for literature (1973).

Emanuel "Manoly" George Lascaris (August 1912-November 13, 2003), Greek-Egyptian-Australian gentleman

Manoly Lascaris and Patrick White on leave together in Beirut

farmer, companion. Lascaris, who grew up in exile—mostly in Egypt—was a direct descendant of Byzantine emperors.

White returned to England in World War II and joined the Royal Air Force. He was an intelligence officer stationed in Alexandria, Egypt (July 1941), when he went to a party of international gay military men and met Lascaris, his interethnic lover for the next fifty years. It is said that Lascaris was a saint to put up with White's hot-headed and dramatic temper. Lascaris scattered White's ashes in Centennial Park in Sydney, Australia.

BIBLIOGRAPHY

Marr, David (1992). *Patrick White: A Life.* New York: Alfred A. Knopf.

MAGNUS HIRSCHFELD AND KARL GIESE AND LIU SHIU TONG AND ERWIN HANSEN

Karl Giese and Magnus Hirschfeld in exile

Dr. Magnus Hirschfeld (May 14, 1868-May 14, 1935), German physician, humanitarian, pioneer sexologist, writer, activist, educator. Hirschfeld's innumerable contributions to social welfare span five continents over half of a century. Hirschfeld is the grandpapa of the modern gay rights movement.

Born in Kolberg on the Baltic Sea to a prominent Jewish family of physicians, Hirschfeld was groomed for a life of polite service to the public. After completing his tour of military service (1891) he returned to medical school. Understanding that his medical credential was key to accomplishing his true interests, he wrote (May 25, 1928):

I gave up the study of philology and literature for biology and medicine for practical reasons only. My true inclination had always been, and still is, to spend my life in the society of journalists, writers, poets and artists. They are much closer to me than physicians and the whole hierarchy of medical science. The natural sciences have always left aside the most important aspect of life, which is love. It has been left to the artist and writer. And I decided to make this theme the mainspring of my medical research. (Wolff, 1986, p. 27)

Hirschfeld founded the Scientific Humanitarian Committee (1897), the first public social agency to advocate for the civil rights of homosexuals and other gender-variant people. The goals were to eradicate criminal statutes found in the German penal code against male homosexuality (Paragraph 175) and abortion (Paragraph 218), and to promote women's suffrage, birth and population control, and treatment for alcoholism. This venue brought previously disparate German gay men and lesbians, together with feminists and social reformers, to a new political clout. The Committee published a Yearbook (1899-1923), and their motto was *Per Scientiam ad Justitiam* (Justice Through Science).

Hirschfeld bought a palace in Berlin (1919) and thus founded the Institute for Sexual Science. The Biedermeier decor and lavishness lent unquestioning credibility to the many in-residence physicians, psychotherapists, marriage counselors, and sexologists. The Institute also had laboratories for research in all forms of human sexuality: domiciles (including those of Hirschfeld and his lover); apartments for the constant stream of visiting artists and dignitaries; and sanctuary "for the down and outs who needed a refuge from the law." But perhaps the most important properties of the Institute were the museum, archives, and library.

At this time little is known of Karl Giese (unknown-March 1938), German archivist, lecturer, radical activist. Giese and Hirschfeld probably met during the first year of the Institute. Witness testimony alludes to their faithful, loving, out-of-the-closet intergenerational relationship that endured to the end. Their interethnic relationship was emblematic during the rise of Nazism: Giese was an Aryan, Hirschfeld a Jew. Contrary to Magnus's short, stocky, butch, sometimes unkempt, genteel demeanor, Karl was tall, thin, femme, fastidious, and campy.

Christopher Isherwood stayed at the Institute and in his autobiography *Christopher and His Kind* (1976) described Karl Giese as follows:

The atmosphere of Karl's sitting room had none of the Institute's noble seriousness; it was a cozy little nest, lined with photographs and souvenirs.

In repose, Karl's long handsome face was melancholy. But soon he would be giggling and rolling his eyes. Touching the back of his head with his fingertips, as if patting bobbed curls, he would strike an It-Girl pose. This dedicated earnest intelligent campaigner for sexual freedom had an extraordinary innocence at such moments. Christopher saw in him the sturdy peasant youth with a girl's heart who, long ago, had fallen in love with Hirschfeld, his father image. Karl still referred to Hirschfeld as "Papa." (Wolff, 1986, p. 186)

And later: "Nearly all the friends who looked in on Karl in the afternoon were middle-class queens. They had a world of their own which included clubs for dancing and drinking" (p. 186).

Hirschfeld was no one's fool. He wrote in "Natural Laws of Love" (1912), "Sex tends to polygamy, while love tends to monogamy" (p. 187).

Hirschfeld had a penchant for femmes and specifically transvestitism, but scholars still disagree about some aspects of his sexuality. Giese, however, preferred exploring the ecstatic rites of flagellation. An employee at the Institute, Erwin Hansen, was a former army gymnastics instructor and Karl's whipmaster. Hirschfeld was aware and encouraging of their special friendship.

As the Nazis rose to power, the Institute was under greater threat. Hirschfeld was attacked on the streets of Munich (1921) by anti-Semites: they fractured his skull and left him for dead. At a lecture he was giving in Vienna (February 4, 1923), Nazi youth hurled stink bombs onto the stage and then opened fire on the audience. By 1930 it was apparent that some employees of the Institute were Nazi sympathizers, members, and spies. Giese, the chief archivist and collector of much of the museum's large array of sexual paraphernalia, started the evacuation of treasures to Paris (1931-1932).

By March 1933, trouble was imminent. Head librarian Röser held the only key to the library and proudly sported a swastika on his lapel.

Nazi mandate now allowed no one in or out of the Institute. According to Günter Maeder, an employee held prisoner, while looking out the window during "the occupation" he saw Giese slip in past the Nazi guard, walk across the courtyard, break into the library by smashing down the door, and heroically escape through SS surveillance, rescuing archival material.

On May 6, 1933, the Nazis finally raided the Institute, carting off more than 10,000 volumes and countless artifacts, including a bronze bust of Hirschfeld. All was incinerated at the auto-da-fé of May 10, 1933. Hirschfeld witnessed this via newsreel weeks later during his exile in Paris.

While Giese had remained in Berlin to salvage archives, Hirschfeld was traveling the world accompanied by his new lover, Liu Shiu Tong. Tao—as everyone called him—was a twenty-three-year-old student of philosophy, sexology, and medicine at the American St. John University in Shanghai when he met Hirschfeld (sixty-three), who was giving a lecture. Tao must have been a perfect femme for Hirschfeld because they were inseparable for the next four years until Hirschfeld died of a stroke on his birthday, while in exile in France. His ashes are interred in Nice at Cauçade Cemetery. In his eulogy, Giese said of Hirschfeld, "He was a gentle fanatic" (Wolff, 1986, p. 414).

Giese, suffering from ill health, committed suicide in March 1938.

Tao left Europe for Hong Kong in 1958. His whereabouts are unknown.

BIBLIOGRAPHY

Wolff, Charlotte (1986). *Magnus Hirschfeld: A Portrait of a Pioneer in Sexology.* London: Quartet Books.

Chapter 6

Pattern of Utopian Love

without warning

as a whirlwind
swoops on an oak
love shakes my heart

Sappho
(Barnard, 1966, p. 44)

Utopian love is a relationship of four or more people who romantically pursue the quixotic goal of the perfect social, political and/or spiritual life, by living, working, and loving together.

People tend to point to utopian communities and say, "See? It didn't last." But in reality, all loves die, eventually. Love is a magic spark that can ignite a fire of passion and romance, a fire that will sooner or later be extinguished by death, divorce, or circumstance. This does not mean that the love was a failure. Loves have their own life spans. The utopian lovers I present here were/are all successful.

Keep in mind that these utopian lovers, for the most part, are alienated from the ways of the world as they know it to be. They are outsiders who struggle to find meaning in life and sanctuary in a world of despair. The selection of utopian lovers that follows is merely a representative sampling of the infinite ways in which queer people form community. This pattern exists in many cultures globally, and a complete accounting is beyond the scope of this book. From Bloomsbury to the 1880s' collective of queer men in Chicago called Spirit Fruit Community, **Sappho**'s school for girls, and radical faerie communes of today (Zuni Mountain Sanctuary, Wolf Creek, Short Mountain Sanctuary), observant historians can find queer community in the stories of revolution everywhere.

Legacies of Love: A Heritage of Queer Bonding
© 2008 by The Haworth Press, Taylor & Francis Group. All rights reserved.
doi:10.1300/5890_07

101

The Anglo-American pirates of the early eighteenth century created democratic codes of honor, freed slaves and indentured servants, and fought against the tyranny of imperialist globalization. They founded an enclave in the Caribbean where queers could be free from religious persecution. Hull House was the first "community services center" in American history. Founded by lesbians, this magnificent settlement house offered assistance to immigrants, women, children, the poor, and other people in need. Men Dancers, the first all-male American dance troupe, was an experiment in how gay men and straight men can live together in peace and creativity. Theatricum Botanicum brought together people of all ages and sexual orientations through the celebration of theater, politics, and gardening. The Shield Society is the result of one man's passion as a samurai to protect the nobility in modern Japan by reinvigorating and creating an army of lovers. Camp Sister Spirit is an example of lesbians providing safe haven for women escaping violent situations.

PIRATES OF THE CARIBBEAN: ANNE BONNY AND MARY READ AND CALICO JACK AND PIERRE THE PANSY PIRATE

Eighteenth-century engraving attributed to Anne Bonny

For a brief but glorious moment in history (1716-1726), the high seas were alive and burgeoning with more than 4,000 Anglo-American pirates. Global mobility for most everyone occurred with the onset of transoceanic trade. Both cargo and passenger ships were circling the globe, bringing food and fine goods to the highest bidders. Empires were being built, much of Europe was at war, America was still only colonies of imperialism, slavery was a booming business, and women were property and had no civil rights. In fact, most people had no rights. Young men were rounded up from prisons or abducted from city streets,

Eighteenth-century engraving attributed to Mary Read and Anne Bonny

and forced to work without pay on cargo and slave ships that greatly prospered a few men: the ship owner, captain, middlemen. Some young men were allowed to work on these ships as a means of getting somewhere. The conditions were horrible and unsanitary, and the exploitation of flesh was rampant.

Sailing under the Jolly Roger, most Anglo-American pirates had a strong fraternal bond with one another; this was often something that had been previously missing in their lives. Most of these pirates joined up when the ships they were working or imprisoned on were pirated; for some it was their first taste of freedom from tyranny. Pirate codes were very strict and somewhat universal. Captains were democratically elected by majority, and were replaceable at any impromptu election. They had to share the captain's quarters. Booty was split equitably among all. These were egalitarian organizations, kin to a utopian community.

In the Bahaman island of New Providence was a queer mecca, a San Francisco, if you will, of the early eighteenth century. Captain

Jack Rackham, aka Calico Jack, worked his way across the Atlantic as a cabin boy/lover of the ship's captain. In New Providence he met Pierre the Pansy Pirate, who ran a local eatery. Pierre also was a hairdresser, but he was most notorious for his haute couture. Pierre was a voluptuary who always had the finest silks and velvets to be found in the New World. He created elaborate costumes for citizens and pirates alike. The loud, multicolored pants he designed for Captain Rackham gave Calico Jack his name.

Anne Cormac was a tomboy who beat up anyone in her way. She left Charleston, South Carolina, to elope with (disreputable) James Bonny. Disinherited, she burned down her father's plantation, and the Bonnys fled to New Providence. Anne Bonny soon dumped her husband ("He's of no use to me") and entered into a ménage à trois with Captain Jennings and his mistress Meg. Bonny left them to marry the richest man on the island, and then left *him* for Calico Jack. It is believed that Bonny and Rackham had a baby, which they gave away.

Mary Read was born in England while her mother's husband had been at sea for two years. To save her honor and ensure her inheritance, Mary's mother dressed her in her newly deceased brother Mark's clothes, and raised her as a boy. Mary/Mark was wild and unruly, filling the bill of a boy so much that her mother wanted to be rid of her. Mark signed up to work on a Dutch merchantman, a ship that was overtaken by Anglo-American pirates whose home port was New Providence. Mark joined the colorful pirates and sailed for her new queer home.

Their tales of adventure are the stuff of dreams: Calico Jack and Pierre the Pansy Pirate, Mary/Mark Read and her lover Anne Bonny the fearless. These marvelous anecdotes are too numerous to recount them all: pirating French ships for fabrics, outmanuevering the Royal British Navy, setting slaves free, being drunk with rum and riches. But perhaps the most frequently recounted tale is that of their final capture.

At their trial in St. Jago de la Vega the entire crew was found guilty of piracy and sentenced to be hanged. When they were asked if there was any reason that they should be spared, only Anne and Mary spoke up: "Your Honor, we plead our bellies." Confirming their pregnancies was the court doctor, a man whom these pirates had rescued from the rack of the prison ship *Jewel* a year earlier. Calico and Pierre were hanged. Mary died of a fever in prison. Anne Bonny's whereabouts are unknown.

BIBLIOGRAPHY

Johnson, Charles (1725). *A General History of the Pirates.*

Rediker, Marcus (1987). *Between the Devil and the Deep Blue Sea: Merchant Seamen, Pirates, and the Anglo-American Maritime World, 1700-1750.* Cambridge: Cambridge University Press.

Thompson, C. J. (1974). *The Mysteries of Sex: Women Who Posed as Men and Men Who Impersonated Women.* New York: Causeway Books.

HULL HOUSE: JANE ADDAMS AND ELLEN GATES STARR AND MARY ROZET SMITH

Jane Addams (September 6, 1860-May 21, 1935), American social worker. Addams was born into an abolitionist household and was nourished in the spirit of political reform. She avoided an arranged marriage (1886). Addams went to college at Rockford Female Seminary where she met (1877) a fellow student, Ellen Gates Starr (March 19, 1859-February 10, 1940), American activist, organizer. Addams and Starr traveled to Europe (1883-1885, 1887-1888) where they observed public coping skills for moderns in the Industrial Age. Their idea of a settlement house was born.

In Chicago, Starr had been a teacher at an elite girl's school. With these affluent connections, Addams and Starr purchased a decaying mansion at the corner of Polk and Halstead Streets named Hull House (September 18, 1889). For more than forty years, Hull House gained an international reputation as the finest example of modern urban welfare. By 1893 Hull House was serving 2,000 visitors per week. They offered classes, day care, a variety of alternating activities, rooms for research, and dispensaries for the needy. Hull House is responsible for having implemented child labor laws, regulations for working women, labor unions, protection for immigrants, mandatory education for children, and industrial safety requirements; improving welfare procedures and women's suffrage; and the establishment of the nation's first juvenile court (1899). Starr was a small woman weighing only 100 pounds, but size did not stop this "radical militant" from being arrested (1914) for interfering with a police officer during a restaurant workers' strike. Starr secured funding to add onto Hull House an art gallery and a theater. Addams served on numerous international committees and received countless awards, notably as the first woman to receive an honorary degree from Yale (1910), and the first American woman to win the Nobel Peace Prize (1931). She donated her Nobel money to the Women's International League for Peace and Freedom. Addams co-founded the American Civil Liberties Union (1920), and was expelled from the Daughters of the American Revolution (1917). Addams authored a dozen books, notably *Democracy and Social Ethics* (1902), *The Spirit of Youth and the City Streets* (1909), *Twenty Years at Hull House* (1910), and *The Second Twenty Years at Hull House* (1930).

In 1890, Jane Addams met Mary Rozet Smith (December 23, 1868-1933), American activist, philanthropist. Smith moved into Hull House and joined as an overlapping and utopian lover. She remained Addams' faithful companionate lover, sharing her bed for forty-three years. These women traveled quite often, especially in America and Europe. They never married, all retaining the title "Miss." Whenever traveling, Addams would always wire ahead to arrange for one double bed. Smith bought a home in Maine (1904), where they spent almost every summer.

Ellen Gates Starr is buried at the Convent of the Holy Child in Suffern, New York. Jane Addams is buried in her native Cedarville, Illinois.

MEN DANCERS:
TED SHAWN AND BARTON MUMAW

America's God will dance, and does dance. I know it, for I am American and my God dances.

Ted Shawn
Gods Who Dance

Ted Shawn (1891-January 9, 1972), American dancer, choreographer, utopian. While studying to be a Methodist minister in Denver, Shawn suffered partial paralysis as a result of diphtheria. Through the new science of dance movement therapy, Shawn found his calling, one that would change American dance forever.

Shawn married Ruth St. Denis (1915), and they merged their two dance academies into the famous Denishawn Company. It was school

Ted Shawn and Barton Mumaw at Jacob's Pillow, 1932

to many later choreographers, most notably Martha Graham. They believed that all dance was sacred. The polarity of American prejudice was that dance was either ballet, which was European in origin, or modern dance, which was woman-identified, leaving little room for creative male movement. Shawn and St. Denis separated in 1930 and remained friends.

Barton Mumaw (August 20, 1912-June 18, 2001), American dancer. As a young trained dancer, Mumaw joined up with Shawn as intergenerational lover and collaborator. They moved to the Berkshire Mountains in Massachusetts and purchased a run-down eighteenth century farmhouse situated on 150 acres. The homestead was known as Jacob's Pillow. It had no running water, electricity, or heat. During the Depression, Shawn and Mumaw marshaled together young male athletes—including a pole-vaulter and a wrestler—who had no dance experience, and formed a utopia called Men Dancers (March 1933-1940). Jess Meeker joined up as the pianist and musical director for this, the first all-male American dance company.

Many of the Men Dancers were/are heterosexual. Some were/are homosexual. More important is their strong same-gender bond of companionship, the dear love of comrades. Shawn had them perform "men's work," digging and ploughing and planting seeds, building stone walls and new buildings. He wanted to avoid urban technology and did not allow radios or telephones. He believed that working together gave them great power. They danced in the mornings and did men's work in the afternoons. After lunch they gathered around as Papa Shawn lectured and read to the men literature and philosophy. One heterosexual Men Dancer recalls: "We were like an Indian tribe" (Honsa, 1986).

Papa Shawn reads the classics to Men Dancers and guest students

Being both pacifists and patriots, Shawn served in the U.S. military (1917-1918) during World War I, as did Mumaw (1942-1945) in World War II. Mumaw recalled that between 1932 and 1941 he was never separated from his lover for more than twenty-four hours at a time.

Before his death Ted Shawn said:

The art of the Dance is too big to be encompassed by any one system, school or style. On the contrary, the Dance includes every way that men of all races in every period of the world's history have moved rhythmically to express themselves.

BIBLIOGRAPHY

Afterdark, August, 1975.

Charmoli, Tony. Personal communication, October 26, 1994.

Felciano, Rita, *Bay Guardian*, February 17, 1993.

Honsa, Ron (1986). "The Men Who Danced." Dance Horizons Video, Princeton Book Company, New Jersey.

Shawn, Ted (1929). *Gods Who Dance*. New York: E. P. Dutton & Company.

Sherman, Jane and Mumaw, Barton (1986). *Barton Mumaw, Dancer: From Denishawn to Jacob's Pillow and Beyond*. New York: Dance Horizons.

THEATRICUM BOTANICUM: WILL GEER AND RALEIGH

Will Auge Geer (March 9, 1902-April 22, 1978), American actor, activist, horticulturist. Geer made his Broadway debut in *The Merry Wives of Windsor* (1928), and starred as Abraham Lincoln in *A Portrait of Lincoln* at Carnegie Hall (1943).

By 1948, Geer was well-established in Hollywood, but he was blacklisted in 1951 for refusing to cooperate with McCarthy's House

Will Geer and Raleigh, 1977

Un-American Activities Committee: he appeared to testify wearing a purple shirt. Geer returned to Broadway for work, and then back again to Hollywood (1962), where he is perhaps best remembered for his role as "Grandpa" on the television series *The Waltons.*

In 1936, Geer married Herta Ware. He had three children with her. He maintained his heterogendered marriage through several overlapping relationships. Geer was an ardent gardener and lifelong student of plants. He founded in Topanga Canyon a botanical utopian community of actors called Theatricum Botanicum—complete with a public theater. The main caretaker and groundskeeper of Theatricum Botanicum was Raleigh (né Roland Meyers, c. 1941–), American spiritualist, actor. At Will's suggestion, Roland dropped out of an Augustinian monastery (1959), changed his name, and was legally adopted as a son by Geer. Raleigh was also a Colt model. When asked about his intergenerational relationship with Geer, Raleigh said they had a "spiritual bond," and that Theatricum Botanicum was his "utopian planetary ministry" (Dougherty, 1983, p. A-12). Geer had many lovers of both genders, notably gay-American civil rights pioneer

Harry Hay. At Geer's funeral, Hay blurted out to Ware, "I had him first." She replied, "I had him longest" (Timmons, 1990, p. 289). His ashes were buried at Theatricum Botanicum.

BIBLIOGRAPHY

Dougherty, Steven, "Long-Winded Legal War Over Will Geer's Will." *Los Angeles Herald Examiner,* January 16, 1983.
Stone, Judy, "To the Devil and Back with Will Geer." *The New York Times,* December 17, 1972.
Timmons, Stuart (1990). *The Trouble with Harry Hay.* Boston: Alyson.

TATE NO KAI (THE SHIELD SOCIETY): YUKIO MISHIMA AND MASAKATSU MORITA

Yukio Mishima (né Kimitake Hiraoka, January 14, 1925-November 25, 1970), Japanese samurai, writer, aesthete, bodybuilder. Mishima was a frail, skinny child, sensitive and dominated by his grandmother. Paternally from peasant stock, Mishima's mother was from an educated family of the samurai class, which instilled in him a great quest for Japanese classical literature. Mishima was also a devotee of homosexual Western writers: **Oscar Wilde,** Marcel Proust, **Jean Cocteau,** and especially **Raymond Radiguet.** The conflict of polarities is perhaps the most dominant theme of Mishima's life.

Mishima was first published at nineteen, and by age twenty-three was celebrated as the greatest Japanese writer of the twentieth century. In all, he wrote forty novels, eighteen plays (all lavishly produced), twenty volumes of short stories and twenty volumes of essays. Mishima was also an actor and director (stage and film), an accomplished swordsman, and an avid bodybuilder, and he conducted a symphony. He traveled around the globe seven times, and was three times nominated for a Nobel Prize.

In post-war Tokyo, gay bars were opening up for the first time in perhaps 200 years. Mishima began hanging out in the Ginza at a gay coffee house/cabaret called the Brunswick (1950). He visited gay clubs around the world and was never closeted about it. Samurai tradition, which Mishima greatly aspired to, requires marriage and the production of male offspring, with extra-dyadic homoerotic partnerships. Mishima wed his beautiful, hip, and sophisticated Yoko (1958), who bore him two children.

Mishima believed in unwavering devotion to the emperor. He abhorred the post-war condition banning a military. He feared the growing left-wing radicals of the 1960s who were espousing communist ideology, and the growing right wing of fascism. But mostly he was troubled morally by the waning adoration for the monarchy. In response he formed a private army to protect the emperor and uphold traditional samurai values. Mishima formed the *Tate no Kai* (Shield Society) with 100 men. They had boot camp and paramilitary training; they exercised, ate, slept, and shared libidinous caprices together in honorable tradition. Mishima's first in command was his lover, Masakatsu Morita. I regret not having more information on Morita, and look forward to recovering his story.

On November 25, 1970, Mishima, Morita, and three other officers of the Shield Society took over the office of the General of the Japanese Self-Defense Forces. They bound and gagged the general, barricaded themselves inside, and demanded that the entire Force appear below for a speech, which Mishima was about to deliver. The Incident had been planned for more than a year, but a few unpredicted problems arose. The crowds booed Mishima and were unable to hear his plea for a greater military and for devotion to the emperor. He cut his lecture short and reentered the General's office for his final act. Mishima first, and then Morita, performed the ancient rite of seppuku, and were then beheaded by Shield Society comrade Hiromasa "Furu" Koga.

Perhaps a biography of Mishima would be incomplete, at least traditionally, without speculation as to why Mishima made such a dramatic suicide sans any note or explanation. In samurai tradition, his was an "honorable death." Yoko is quoted as saying that it was the first thing her husband did in his life that he was truly content with. Others have referred to his fascination with homoerotic sadomasochism and his infatuation with martyrdom. It is my opinion that Mishima believed in the traditional Japanese concept of the "death mask." He was forty-five years old and peaking in the sculpting of his body. He would therefore carry with him into eternity the death mask (and body) of a strong, powerful, and courageous samurai warrior.

BIBLIOGRAPHY

Nathan, John (1974). *Mishima: A Biography.* Boston: Little, Brown & Company.

CAMP SISTER SPIRIT:
WANDA HENSON AND BRENDA HENSON

Wanda Henson (November 21, 1954–) and Brenda Henson (September 25, 1945–), American feminists, utopians. Wanda and Brenda met January 14, 1984, while defending an abortion clinic from anti-choice zealots in Mississippi. The Hensons were both previously married to men, each with two children. But they fell in love, moved in together, and created many projects to empower women. In November 1993, the not-for-profit organization they co-founded, Sister Spirit Incorporated, purchased a 120-acre pig farm in Ovett, Mississippi, with the intention of creating a feminist education retreat.

Brenda and Wanda Henson at wedding

Wanda (a nurse practitioner) and Brenda both hold graduate degrees in adult education.

Camp Sister Spirit is now a safe haven for women supporting women, the LGBT community, and others who support equality. They offer a food bank and a clothing exchange program, counseling services, and a rural retreat for nourishing the spirits of women and others.

Camp Sister Spirit soon became the target of misogynist and homophobic neighbors. The women at Camp Sister Spirit have been shot at and received death threats, and have been the victims of vandalism. The local bigots even hung a dead puppy from the mailbox of Camp Sister Spirit. But the women are strong and will not be shaken. They are armed and patrol their property in pairs, twenty-four hours a day. Setting a precedent, gender-variant United States Attorney General Janet Reno sent a special envoy of mediators in attempts to quell the homophobic terrorism in Ovett, Mississippi.

After the catastrophe of Hurricane Katrina, Camp Sister Spirit became a focal point for relief efforts in their section of Mississippi, supplying hundreds of citizens with tons of food, water, and clothing. Today, Camp Sister Spirit is a vital part of the little Ovett, Mississippi, community, and many townsfolk who previously hated them now protectively refer to these sacred sisters as "our lesbians."

Brenda and Wanda Henson with marriage license in Massachusetts

BIBLIOGRAPHY

Chesler, Phyllis. "Sister, Fear Has No Place Here." *On The Issues,* Fall 1994.

Pharr, Suzanne. "Rural Organizing: Building Community Across Difference." *Sojourner: The Woman's Journal,* June 1994.

SAPPHO AND ATTHIS

Sappho (c. 612-c. 560 BCE), Lesbian poet, educator. Born in Eresos on the island of Lesbos, Sappho is thus far the earliest recorded lesbian in Western culture. Her lyric poetry was compiled in nine books of 330 stanzas, written in her Aeolic dialect. Plato referred to Sappho as "The Tenth Muse."

After her brief exile to Sicily, Sappho returned to Lesbos, where, some sources say, she founded an educational and cultural center for young women. This academy attracted noble pupils from throughout the Hellenic world. It is speculated that these maidens were groomed in the arts of poetry, music, dance, and love, which were then practiced in secret all-girl rites.

At the end of the Middle Ages, the Catholic Church, in its anti-romantic doctrine, ordered all of Sappho's texts destroyed. In the beginning of the twentieth century, in a cave in Turkey, remains were found of an ancient wine jug, which had been stopped up with a sheath of papyrus. On this papyrus were some of Sappho's poems, with fragments missing where the acid of the wine had eaten away at the Egyptian paper. Atthis is the subject of some of Sappho's love poem fragments.

Chapter 7

Pattern of Peer Love

No power in heaven, hell or earth can separate us, for our hearts
are eternally wedded together.

Elizabeth Cady Stanton
to Susan B. Anthony
(Banner, 1980)

Peer love is a relationship between two same-gender persons of
equal class status, same ethnicity, and nine years or less age difference. Peer lovers are "the norm," representing approximately 55 to 60
percent of gay and lesbian lovers.

HARMODIUS
AND ARISTOGEITON

Harmodius (c. 530 BCE-c. 514 BCE)
and Aristogeiton (c. 530 BCE-c. 514 BCE),
Greek patriots, tyrannicides. While Athens
was under the unpopular tyranny of Hippias, the ruler's brother, Hipparchus, made
unseemly sexual advances toward Harmodius. Harmodius and his lover Aristogeiton
plotted to rid their country of these bullies.
But Hippias escaped the assassination attempt that took his brother's life, and that of
Harmodius. Aristogeiton was executed
shortly thereafter. Hippias was finally expelled from Athens (510 BCE), whereby

Harmodius and Aristogeiton

Legacies of Love: A Heritage of Queer Bonding
© 2008 by The Haworth Press, Taylor & Francis Group. All rights reserved.
doi:10.1300/5890_08

Harmodius and Aristogeiton were turned into folk heroes with coins struck in their image and statues erected. Festivals were celebrated in their honor for several centuries.

DUKE LING OF WEI AND NI XIA

Duke Ling of Wei (534-493 BCE), Chinese monarch. Ni Xia (unknown), Chinese minister. These two lovers were strolling in a peach orchard one day, when Ni picked a ripe fruit from a tree. The peach was so sweet that he offered it to the duke. To this day, a common euphemism in China for male-male love is *fen tao zhi ai,* meaning "the love of shared peach."

MARY WOLLSTONECRAFT AND FRANCES BLOOD

Mary Wollstonecraft (April 27, 1759-September 10, 1797), English writer, feminist. Wollstonecraft authored *Vindication of the Rights of Women* (1792), considered the first great feminist document. Wollstonecraft spent most of her life being romantically in love with Frances "Fanny" Blood (c. 1757-November 29, 1785), English feminist. She wore a locket with a lock of Fanny's hair in it. They opened a school together (1783). In 1788, Wollstonecraft wrote *Mary,* a novel about her relationship with Fanny. They may have never engaged in sexual interaction, but their extant passionate letters are indisputable evidence of their passionate love.

In 1785, Fanny married Hugh Skeys and they moved to Lisbon. Wollstonecraft went to visit them as Fanny prepared to deliver. Fanny died in her arms during childbirth. Wollstonecraft later lived in Paris during the Revolution with her American lover Gilbert Imlay. After she gave birth to their daughter, Fanny (1794), he deserted her. She later married William Godwin (1797). In the same year, Wollstonecraft died while giving birth to daughter Mary, who later became the author of *Frankenstein* and wife of homosexual poet Percy Bysshe Shelley.

BIBLIOGRAPHY

Tomalin, Claire (1974). *The Life and Death of Mary Wollstonecraft.* New York: Harcourt Brace Jovanovich.

QUEEN ANNE AND SARAH CHURCHILL

Queen Anne   Sarah Churchill, Duchess of Marlborough

Anne (February 6, 1665-August 1, 1714), English queen. Anne was the Queen of England, Scotland, and Ireland (1702-1707), Queen of Great Britain and Ireland (1707-1714), and was known as "Good Queen Anne." Anne was fortunate to rule the British Isles in a time of great scientific, philosophic, artistic, and political progress. Anne's sister, Mary II, Queen of England, Scotland, and Ireland (1689-1694), was a lesbian, and was passionately in love with Frances Apsley, who was placed into a marriage of accommodation with Anne's homosexual cousin William (III) of Orange. Anne's arranged marriage (July 28, 1683) to Prince George of Denmark was lovingly companionate and sexual, but unfruitful. All of their seventeen children died, most in infancy. The child who lived to be the oldest was William, the Duke of Gloucester, who died at age eleven (1700).

Sarah Jennings Churchill (1660-1744), English aristocrat, Duchess of Marlborough. When Anne was nine and Sarah fourteen, they were intimate friends. Their very close relationship would last most of their lives, Sarah undoubtedly being the most influential person on Anne during her popular reign. Their passionate love is well-documented in their numerous extant letters to each other, discreetly addressed to Anne as "Mrs. Morley," and to Sarah as "Mrs. Freeman."

Sarah's arranged marriage (c. 1677) to warrior John Churchill was convenient due to his regular absences, which left Sarah alone at court with Anne. Queen Anne was generous to Sarah and John with her bequeathal of titles, properties, and goods.

A political struggle in England between the Tories and the Whigs over the finances of war, coupled with Anne's shifting of some power from the monarchy to cabinet responsibility, led to a falling-out between Anne and her opinionated lover Sarah and Sarah's military husband (1708). But personal issues were also coincidental: Anne was now having an affair with Sarah's cousin, Abigail Hill Masham. It is said that at this time Queen Anne and Lady Churchill had loud vexatious squabbles in public about their relationship, outing each other to the world.

Sarah left most of her vast fortune to her "first woman" Grace Ridley.

CONRADIN AND FREDERICK OF BADEN

Conradin (March 25, 1252-October 29, 1268), German royal. Orphaned at age two, Conradin became the Duke of Swabia and the titular king of Jerusalem and of Sicily. He left Bavaria at age fourteen, crossing the Alps into Italy. There he rallied Italian forces in an attempt to expel French invaders from his Italian provinces. After several successful engagements, Conradin was captured. The French tried him for treason and sentenced him, at age sixteen, to be beheaded. His lover, Frederick of Baden, volunteered to be executed alongside him. Their remains lie together at the monastery of Santa Maria del Carmine in Naples.

ANNE LOUISE GERMAINE DE STAËL
AND JULIETTE RÉCAMIER

They were the most famous women of their time. French socialites Anne Louise Germaine de Staël (1767-July 13, 1817) and Juliette Récamier (December 4, 1777-1849) first met in 1798 during Napoleon's reconstruction of France after the Revolution. They were the epicenter of thought in Parisian society for two decades. De Staël was a prolific writer of romance novels, plays, and critiques of social in-

Germaine de Stâel, portrait by Gérard   Juliette Récamier, portrait by Gérard

stitutions. She was better known, however, for her wit, sharp tongue, loquaciousness, and originality of thought. Her gift of gab was so severe it was reported that she could wear anyone out; her elocutionary discourse persisted for hours on end. De Staël was not considered to be highly attractive. She was referred to publicly in less than attractive terms. Although de Staël was married and had three children, she was perhaps the most accomplished sexual athlete in all of France. Her liaisons with both men and women were incalculable and acknowledged in public sans any shame.

Récamier, on the other hand, was another story. She was married off at fifteen to the wealthiest banker in Paris, who was fifty. They admitted publicly to the chastity of their relationship, and although Récamier had many sexual relations with women, it wasn't until she was fifty-five that she experienced her first carnal knowledge of a male, with the legendary Vicomte de Chateaubriand. Whereas de Staël was considered the brains of Paris, Récamier was touted as the beauty of Paris. Together they forged an alliance so powerful that

Emperor Napoleon felt threatened. Récamier was famous for her teasing and coquettishness, for titillating aristocratic gentlemen, but never putting out. Her seductive beauty left Napoleon panting and pissed off. He had her entered into his Great Book of Suspects because she wouldn't submit to his sexual requests.

De Staël was too smart, ergo dangerous, so Napoleon had her exiled. She spent most of the rest of her life at her Château de Coppet on Lake Geneva, writing, holding salons, having sex, and consuming opium. Despite her banishment by Napoleon, when she learned of a plot to assassinate him, she warned him in time to save his life. Récamier is buried in Paris at Montmartre.

BIBLIOGRAPHY

Herold, J. Christopher (1959). *Mistress of an Age: The Life of Mme. de Staël.* Bobs-Merrill.

"Juno & The Peacock," *Time,* April 28, 1958.

Levaillant, Maurice (1958). *The Passionate Exiles: A Dual Biography of Mme. Récamier & Mme. de Staël.* Farrar, Straus & Cudahy, Inc.

Nathalie Micas and Rosa Bonheur

ROSA BONHEUR AND NATHALIE MICAS

Marie Rosalie Bonheur (March 16, 1822-May 25, 1899), French painter. Bonheur was celebrated in her life as a great painter of landscapes and animals. She often visited slaughterhouses and butchers, and dissected animals to more fully understand their corporeality. To visit these unseemly places incognito, Bonheur dressed in male attire, obtaining an official *permission de travestissement* (1857). She cut her hair short, smoked cigars, and was once arrested, when she donned a skirt, for impersonating a woman. Bonheur's works were greatly influenced by contemporary bisexual French author George Sand. Her many paintings are in collections in Europe and America (at the Metropolitan in New York and the Corcoran in Washington, DC). Bonheur was the first woman awarded the coveted Grand Cross of the French Legion of Honor. Bonheur self-identified as "contrasexual."

Nathalie-Jeanne Micas (c. 1824-1889), French artist, inventor. Micas was six when she met Bonheur, eight, in 1830. They were lovers and companions for more than forty years. Bonheur was raised in a goddess-worshipping utopian community. Bonheur and Micas eschewed public life in preference for their pastoral, animal-packed life at their Château By. Micas's mother lived with them. On his deathbed, her father blessed her union with Bonheur and implored them to stay together. After Micas's death, Bonheur wrote that she "loved [her] more and more as we advanced in life" (Ashton, 1981, p. 121).

Rosa   Bonheur   and   Anna Klumpke

Shortly after Micas's death, Bonheur was visited by San Franciscan painter Anna Elizabeth Klumpke (1856-1942), who became her lover and biographer. Bonheur bequeathed her fortune to Klumpke. Rosa Bonheur, Nathalie Micas, and Anna Klumpke are all buried together at the Micas family vault in Père Lachaise, Paris.

BIBLIOGRAPHY

Ashton, Dore (1981). *Rosa Bonheur: A Life and a Legend.* New York: Viking.
Marks, Jim, *Washington Blade,* May 29, 1981.
Saslow, James M., "Rosa Bonheur: Allowed to Be Unusual Because She Was Successful." *The Advocate,* September 22, 1976.

CO'PAK

A nineteenth-century recording of a unique woman gives us a fragment of a clue of a gender-variant female's experience. Co'Pak, Klamath *tw!inna'ek* dressed mostly in female attire but "lived like a man. . . . She tried to talk like a man and invariably referred to herself as one." Co'Pak lived with a woman to whom she was married for many years. When her wife died, Co'Pak "observed the usual mourning, wearing a bark belt as a man does at this time" (Williams, 1986, p. 242).

BIBLIOGRAPHY

Williams, Walter L. (1986). *The Spirit and the Flesh: Sexual Diversity in American Indian Culture.* Boston: Beacon Press.

THOMAS ATWOOD AND WILLIAM MINNICH

William Minnich and Thomas Atwood at Harrisburg, 1864

Thomas Van Allen Atwood, twenty-two, and William Watson Minnich, seventeen, posed for this photograph in 1864. They served together in the Union Army where they began their sexual relations and lifelong romance. At the end of the Civil War, Atwood returned to marry his prewar betrothed, a woman named Myrtle. But according to her descendants, he left her sexually unsatisfied. Atwood's lover from the war, William Minnich, came to visit the newlyweds on their farm. Minnich got Myrtle pregnant, and then ran off with her husband/his lover to an exciting life out West. Minnich and Atwood were then together for fifteen years. When Atwood was murdered, Minnich returned to Myrtle to marry his lover's widow.

MARY GREW AND MARGARET BURLEIGH

> Love is spiritual, only passion is sexual.
>
> Mary Grew
> (Smith-Rosenberg, n.d.)

Mary Grew (September 1, 1813-October 10 ,1896), American abolitionist, suffragist. Grew was a founding member of the Female Anti-Slavery Society (1830s) in Philadelphia and active in the American Peace Society. She was co-editor of the abolitionist paper *Pennsylvania Freeman.* Grew worked diligently in the Free Produce Association, a political organization advocating the boycott of slave-grown products. She was the first president of the Pennsylvania Woman Suffrage Association (1869) and presided for twenty-three years.

Grew never married. She lived most of her life with her lover Margaret Burleigh. Grew is buried at Woodlands Cemetery, Philadelphia.

BIBLIOGRAPHY

Marshall, Megan, "The Boston Marriage," *New England Monthly,* December, 1986.
Smith-Rosenberg, Carroll (n.d.). "The Female World of Love and Ritual: Relations Between Women in Nineteenth Century America." *Signs;* Vol. 1, No. 1, University of Chicago Press, pp. 1-29.

JIM GILLIS AND DICK STOKER

Jim Gillis (1830-1907), a confirmed lifetime bachelor, and his "pard," Dick Stoker, were American gold miners. They lived together in a log cabin in Jackass Gulch, California. Their companionate love is evidenced, as are trips to San Francisco. Mark Twain reinterpreted tales of Gillis in *Adventures of Huckleberry Finn* and *A Tramp Abroad.* In his autobiography, Twain writes of visiting this couple:

Jackass Gulch, that serene and reposeful and dreamy and delicious sylvan paradise. . . . Every now and then Jim would have an inspiration and he would stand up before the great log fire, with his back to it and his hands crossed behind him, and deliver himself of an elaborate impromptu lie—a fairy tale, an extravagant romance—with Dick Stoker as the hero of it as a general thing. Jim always soberly pretended that what he was relating was strictly history, veracious history, not romance. Dick Stoker, gray-headed and good-natured, would sit smoking his pipe and listen with a gentle serenity to these monstrous fabrications and never utter a protest. (Neider, 1959, pp. 152-153)

One needn't be much of a miner to read between these heterosexual lines to find the mainline of queer gold. This relationship is estimated to have lasted thirty years.

BIBLIOGRAPHY

Neider, Charles (ed.) (1959). *The Autobiography of Mark Twain*. New York: Harper & Row.

OZAWENDIB AND WAGETOTE

In his autobiography, John Tanner wrote of his life among the Chippewa in the 1820s. He recorded many cases of two-spirit persons in this tribe. One was of a man who dressed and lived as a woman, Ozawendib (The Yellow Head), Chippewa *agokwa*. Tanner claimed that Ozawendib was about fifty years old when she continued to offer him sexual favors if he would take her as a wife. Ozawendib had had many husbands, and eventually left the village in search of a new one. She returned and fetched Tanner to introduce him to her new husband, Wagetote, Chippewa man. Wagetote was considered prosperous, having his own lodge, two female wives, and an *agokwa* wife.

STEPHEN FOSTER AND GEORGE COOPER

Stephen Collins Foster (July 4, 1826-January 13, 1864), American songwriter, composer. Foster was a musically gifted child, but his parents lacked the resources for a formal education. Earlier works demonstrate how influenced he was by African-American folk music and the minstrel shows he frequented. Foster wrote popular songs for twenty years that were sung throughout America. These are standards we still sing today, 150 years later: "Oh! Susanna" (1848), "Camptown Races" (1850), "Jeannie with the Light Brown Hair" (1854), "Beautiful Dreamer" (c. 1864).

Foster was a masculine man who once beat up a band of bullies. He was also sensitive and highly emotional. He was a mama's boy who ran home sobbing to his mother on his wedding night. After years of success, and an ensuing alcohol problem, Foster finally left his wife and daughter to be exclusively homosexual in New York City (1860).

George Cooper (dates unknown), American songwriter. Cooper was a handsome law student whose prearranged life seemed meaningless. He dropped out of school to study poetry and music, whence he fell in love with the famous Stephen Foster. They collaborated on many songs, but the famous barbershop-quartet standard "Sweet Genevieve" is attributed solely to Cooper.

Stephen Foster died of alcoholism at the age of thirty-seven. Cooper cared for Foster during his death, and inherited his last effects: thirty-eight cents. George Cooper, at age thirty-seven, married and began his procreational family. Foster was buried at Allegheny Cemetery, Pittsburgh, Pennsylvania.

Stephen Foster and George Cooper

JAMES BUCHANAN AND WILLIAM RUFUS KING

James Buchanan

James Buchanan (April 23, 1791-June 1, 1868), American president. As the fifteenth president of the United States, Buchanan remains the only bachelor president. A Federalist turned conservative Democrat, Buchanan was a politician who held divergent views. He was against slavery but supported individual states' right to choose slavery, such as in the Kansas decision; he also supported the efforts to purchase Cuba as a slave state. He alienated many people with his conflicting views and was elected president (1857) not by popular majority vote, but due to the unusual circumstances of a three-party split between the Democrats, the newly formed Republican Party, and the teamed-up Whigs and the Know-Nothings. His inability to stave off differences between Northern abolitionists and Southern secessionists led to the presidency of **Abraham Lincoln** and the American Civil War.

William Rufus Devane King (April 7, 1786-April 18, 1853), American senator, vice president. King, also a lifelong bachelor, was a U.S. senator from Alabama (1819-1844, 1848-1852), and was later sworn in as vice president, but died the month after taking office. King has been depicted as effeminate and was dubbed by former president Andrew Jackson as "little Miss Nancy."

Buchanan and King shared an apartment in the capital for sixteen years. It has been asserted that we cannot make assumptions about their relationship solely on the fact that they shared close quarters for a long period, as it wasn't an uncommon practice among diplomats at the time. However, it is this reviewer's opinion that we cannot so lightly dismiss this

William Rufus King

important evidence, especially when accounting for their financial independence, their lack of interest in pursuing females, the ridicule they suffered, and their extant letters of affection. By choosing to stay together, Buchanan and King made a radical statement of legendary companionate love.

ABRAHAM LINCOLN AND JOSHUA SPEED

Abraham Lincoln (February 12, 1809-April 15, 1865), American president. When young Lincoln was working his way through law school, he stopped into a general store in Springfield, Illinois, and he met the proprietor, Joshua Fry Speed (1814-1882), American businessman. We do not know exactly what happened, but we do know that Speed then and there offered Lincoln to share his bed in the small room above the store. These two large men in their early twenties shared a small double bed for four years. They hung out at night with a group of confirmed bachelors who were given to song and telling tales, but Lincoln often preferred to be alone and read poetry.

Abraham Lincoln   Joshua Fry Speed

When Speed sold his store and returned to his wealthy family in Kentucky to oblige an arranged marriage, Lincoln was devastated. Prone to depression, Lincoln became distressed and his melancholy grew worse. Lincoln summoned an MD, who diagnosed him with "hypochondria." Some say that Lincoln never recovered from his abandonment by Speed. As president, Lincoln appointed Speed's brother James as Attorney General, it is said to keep family ties and increase their chances of meeting.

Lincoln did not show up for his wedding the first time, but finally married (some say lesbian) Mary Todd (November 1842). Three of their four children died in childhood (Edward at four, Willie at twelve, Tad at eighteen). Due to these premature deaths and Mary Todd's mental institutionalization (1875), some speculate that the Lincolns were carriers of syphilis.

Abraham Lincoln was assassinated by actor John Wilkes Booth, who many claim was a homosexual.

BIBLIOGRAPHY

Barton, William E. (1928). *Abraham Lincoln and Walt Whitman.* Indianapolis: The Bobbs-Merrill Company.

Kincaid, Robert Lee (1943). *Joshua Fry Speed; Lincoln's Most Intimate Friend.* Harrogate, TN.

Oates, Stephen B. (1977). *With Malice Toward None: The Life of Abraham Lincoln.* New York: Harper & Row.

ALICE FLETCHER AND JANE GAY

Alice Cunningham Fletcher (March 15, 1838-April 6, 1923), Cuban-American ethnologist and Indian rights activist. Early in her life Fletcher was interested in women's issues and Temperance, but it was her fascination with archaeology that led her to anthropology and her lifetime of advocacy for American Indians. Fletcher befriended, studied, and aided many tribes, notably the Omaha, the Pawnee, and the Nez Perce, where she formed a close relationship with Chief Joseph. She transcribed and preserved hundreds of Plains Indian songs and rituals, many never recorded elsewhere, notably the Pawnee *Hako* ceremony (1904). Fletcher was personally responsible for passage of

Alice Fletcher and Emma Jane Gay cooking out

Congressional acts giving choice lands to Indians. She served as the vice president of the Women's Anthropological Society (1885), and was the first woman to join the all-male Anthropology Society of Washington (1899), becoming its president (1903). Fletcher was the founder and charter member of the American Anthropological Association (1902), and president of the American Folklore Society (1905).

Emma Jane Gay (1830-1919), American photographer. Gay held many jobs in her life and moved frequently. With her companion Miss Catherine M. Melville, Gay opened a school for young ladies in Macon, Georgia (1856), but soon moved to the North (1861) to assist her friend Miss Dorothea Dix in caring for Union soldiers. Miss Gay tutored President Johnson's children at the White House (1865).

Gay had left an indelible impression, many years earlier, on her student Alice Fletcher. When they reunited in 1888, Fletcher convinced Gay, fifty-eight, to learn the new art of photography and to accompany her out West to document Indian cultures and the frontier.

In 1893, Gay and Fletcher retired to their home in Washington, DC, a central hub of Indian rights activities for the next twenty years. They received many notable American Indian visitors. A collection of 450 of Gay's photographs is held at the Idaho State Historical Society.

BIBLIOGRAPHY

Harvard Magazine, March/April, 1980, pps. 50-51.
Mark, Joan (1989). *A Stranger in Her Native Land.* Omaha: University of Nebraska Press.

ALICE AUSTEN AND GERTRUDE TATE

Elizabeth Alice Austen (March 17, 1866-June 9, 1952), American photographer. Although she traveled extensively, Austen spent most of her long life living on her grandparents' estate on Staten Island, which is now a museum to this legendary couple. Her uncle brought home a camera when she was a child and built her a darkroom a few years later. When most other women photographers in the latter half of the nineteenth century were romantically portraying young women dancing on tiptoe through flower-filled fields, Austen was on the streets documenting the reality of bold and strong women performing their everyday tasks, and women satirically breaking taboos: smoking cigarettes, exhibiting their bloomers, bicycle riding. She drove an ambulance during World War I.

In 1899, Austen met Gertrude Amelia Tate (August 15, 1871-September 26, 1962), American educator and dance instructor. Their romantic companionship lasted more than fifty years. Together they were tireless adventurers and travelers. They lost their financial security during the stock market crash (1929) and never recovered. Unable to survive on Tate's earnings, they suffered greatly in the end, with Austen being sent to a pauper's shelter. Tate's last wish of being buried with her lover proved unaffordable: she is instead buried in the Tate family plot at Cypress Hills Cemetery. Austen's remains are buried at the Moravian Cemetery, Staten Island.

BIBLIOGRAPHY

Novotny, Ann (1976). *Alice's World.* Connecticut: The Chatham Press.
Novotny, Ann, "Alice Austen's World." *Heresies,* Fall, 1977.

NATALIE BARNEY AND ROMAINE BROOKS

Natalie Clifford Barney (October 31, 1876-February 2, 1972),
American-French socialite, writer. Beatrice Romaine Brooks (May 1,
1874-December 7, 1970), American painter, socialite. Barney and
Brooks may have fallen into obscurity if their large inheritances were
not so legendary. But it is precisely their class privilege that gave
them the opportunity to be open and unapologetically lesbian, setting
a tone for twentieth-century lesbian pride.

Barney was raised merrily, with all the music and art lessons possible. In childhood she was bilingual, speaking French as often as English. Her mother was a painter who studied with James McNeill
Whistler, and was a great patron of the arts. Barney wrote poetry,
plays, memoirs, and more, almost exclusively in French, but she was
never serious about her own writing, and instead was more concerned
about promoting her friends' art. Barney was more in love with the art

Natalie Barney and Romaine Brooks at Geneva, c. 1915

Liane de Pougy and Natalie Barney   Natalie Barney and Renée Vivien

of living than the production of art. She was first "outed" during the
Parisian belle epoque by her lover Liane de Pougy in her thinly dis-
guised novel *Idylle saphique* (c. 1901). Barney was well known as a
seductress, and wins the *Legacies of Love* Most Sexually Active Lesbian Award. Other Barney lovers included Renée Vivien, **Colette,**
Djuna Barnes, Edna St. Vincent Millay, Nancy Cunard, **Sylvia
Beach,** Dolly Wilde (**Oscar Wilde**'s niece), and, of course, Brooks
whom she first met in 1915, and spent the better part of fifty years
with.

Brooks was born Beatrice Romaine Goddard in Rome, and was
shortly thereafter abandoned by her father. Her histrionic mother was
abusive, a loose cannon, and put Romaine in the role of caring for her
severely mentally ill brother. Romaine's childhood was fraught with
instability, being sent from boarding schools to relatives, from opu-
lence to poverty and back. Her superstitious mother forbade her to
paint or sketch. Later, while living on the island of Capri, Brooks established herself as a painter, utilizing bright, vivid colors, which
were déclassé in the marketplace. Her mother died, leaving Romaine
the family fortune and the financial independence she so needed. Her
painting soon changed to mostly portraiture in shades of gray. Her
"ephemeral marriage" to homosexual pianist John Ellingham Brooks
lasted but a few months (1903).

Natalie Barney and Romaine Brooks

Brooks and Barney spent much of their life together at 20 rue Jacob, in Paris, where they held literary salons almost every Friday for fifty years. For safety, they moved to Florence, Italy, during World War II, where Barney—despite being one-quarter Jewish—exalted the efforts of Mussolini and fascism, and expressed her anti-Semitism. Remarkably, after surviving the turn of the century, two World Wars, and more than fifty years of companionship, they became estranged (1969). Barney, ninety-three, had cruised a woman named Janine Lahovary on the beach in Nice. Brooks warned Barney that she'd had enough, and that if Barney hooked up with this stranger at the beach, it would be over. Barney had heard this cry for years, and did not believe it. When she returned to their hotel suite, Brooks was gone. Brooks died within a year, Barney fourteen months later.

BIBLIOGRAPHY

Secrest, Meryle (1974). *Between Me and Life: A Biography of Romaine Brooks.* London: Macdonald and Jane's.

EDITH SOMERVILLE AND VIOLET MARTIN

Edith Anna Oenone Somerville (1861-1949) and Violet Florence Martin (aka Martin Ross) (June 1865-1915), Irish writers. Somerville and Martin were second cousins who met in 1886. They lived together until Martin died. They first collaborated on a novel, *An Irish Cousin* (1889), and together published more than twenty volumes under the joint name Somerville and Ross. Martin used the pseudonym Martin Ross to gain access into the male-dominated industry of publishing. Their book *Irish Memories* (1917) is about their relationship.

Edith Somerville and Violet Martin

WILLA CATHER AND EDITH LEWIS

Willa (née Wilella) Sibert Cather (December 7, 1873-April 24, 1947), American writer. Cather was a tomboy who greatly loved the outdoors and hunting and fishing. She went by the nickname of Willie most of her childhood. She is most noted for her many novels depicting the vanishing American frontier, the difficulty of strong people trapped in small lives, and the dichotomous struggle of the artist in society. Her most famous novels include *O Pioneers!* (1913), *My Ántonia* (1918), Pulitzer Prize–winning *One of Ours* (1922), and *Death Comes for the Archbishop* (1927).

Cather, who never admitted being a lesbian, was reported as having anti-Semitic tendencies and other less savory political beliefs. Almost all of her meaningful relationships were with strong, independent women. Her first romantic affair was at the turn of the century with Louise Pound. In 1901, she moved in with Isabelle McClung's family, and despite the family's great wealth, the two young women shared a bedroom for five years. Isabelle took Willa (1902) on her first trip to Europe, and many excursions followed.

Willa Cather   Edith Lewis, 1902

In Lincoln, Nebraska (1908), Cather met Edith Lewis (unknown-1972), American writer and companion. Lewis was Cather's secretary, housewife, and lifetime companion of thirty-nine years. They lived mostly in New York—Greenwich Village and later (1931) at 570 Park Avenue. Lewis is described as self-effacing, often disappearing into the background. She wrote a biography of her lover, *Willa Cather Living* (1953). On a trip to the Southwest, Cather and Lewis were lost overnight in Mesa Verde Canyon; they were rescued the following day.

Cather and Lewis are buried together in Jaffrey, New Hampshire. Cather's will forbids publishing her letters, turning her books into screenplays, and anthologizing any of her work.

BIBLIOGRAPHY

O'Brien, Sharon (1987). *Willa Cather: The Emerging Voice*. New York: Oxford University Press.
Slotey, Bernice (1973). *Willa Cather, a Pictorial Memoir*. Lincoln: University of Nebraska Press.

EMMA GOLDMAN AND MABEL DODGE LUHAN

Love, the strongest and deepest element in all life, the harbinger of hope, of joy, of ecstasy; love, the defier of all laws, of all conventions; love, the freest, the most powerful molder of human destiny; how can such an all-compelling force be synonymous with that poor little State and Church-begotten weed, marriage?

Emma Goldman
(Goldman, 1911, p. 233)

Emma Goldman in Philadelphia mugshot, 1893

Emma Goldman (June 27, 1869-May 14, 1940), Lithuanian-Russian-American-exile anarchist, activist, lecturer. Goldman is a fiery character in the history of global politics. This bio would undoubtedly piss her off. She had many lovers of both sexes, but never admitted to her same-sex relationships. She advocated for the legal rights of homosexuals, and was instrumental in an international campaign against the policy of **Magnus Hirschfeld** outing prominent people.

Goldman escaped a prearranged marriage by emigrating to America (1885). She married Jacob Kersner (1887), but soon divorced him on the grounds that he was impotent. She said that her life really began when she moved to New York City (1889). Goldman spent one year in prison (1893) after being arrested for a speech she made in Union Square telling unemployed starving people that it was their "sacred right" to steal bread. Goldman is the author of *Anarchism and Other Essays* (1911) and was the co-editor of the magazine *Mother Earth* (1906-1917). In 1916, she was arrested for advocating birth control via the magazine. She spent another two years in prison (1917-1919) for publicly inciting opposition to conscription. Upon her release, **J. Edgar Hoover** ordered Goldman to be deported back to Russia. She then moved to Sweden and Germany, where she wrote *My Disillusionment in Russia* (1923). To obtain British citizenship, Emma Goldman married James Colton (1925).

Mabel Luhan (née Ganson, February 26, 1879-August 13, 1962), American heiress, seeker. Mabel was born with everything in her upper-class Buffalo, New York, mansion—everything but a self. She passed her life searching for meaning and purpose, always collecting provocative and famous people, but never feeling a part of anything until she moved to Taos, New Mexico. Mabel was primarily heterosexual and had four husbands: Karl Evans (1900); Edwin Dodge (1905), with whom she lived in Florence and entertained **Gertrude Stein**; Maurice Sterne (1917); and Tony Luhan (1923), a Taos Pueblo native. While living in New York (1912), ever the experimenter, Mabel entertained queers, mystics, and radicals at her famous salons. Perhaps her most notable acquaintance was lesbian American reproductive rights advocate Margaret Sanger. It is here where Mabel met her lover, Emma Goldman. Little is known of their short-lived affair. Luhan wrote a memoir, *Background* (1933).

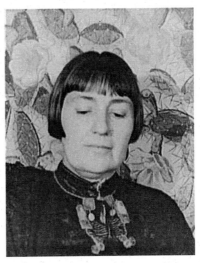

Mabel Dodge Luhan

BIBLIOGRAPHY

Goldman, Emma (1911). *Anarchism and Other Essays.* New York and London: Mother Earth Publishing Assoc.

MARGUERITE YOURCENAR AND GRACE FRICK

Marguerite Antoinette Jeanne Marie Ghislaine Cleenewerck (née de Crayencour) Yourcenar (June 8, 1903-December 17, 1987), Belgian-American writer. Yourcenar was an erudite scholar of Latin and Greek classics, composing most of her poetry, novels, and plays in French. Many of her literary works are about male homosexual love, notably *Mishima: A Vision of the Void* (1981) and *Memoirs of Hadrian* (1951). Among her many awards were the French Commander of the Legion of Honor, and after 346 years of male separatism, Yourcenar was the first woman to be elected and immortalized in the *Académie Française.*

Grace Frick (d. 1979), American translator. Frick translated most of Yourcenar's works into English. Frick was noted as an accomplished equestrian. She and Yourcenar were lovers for forty years; they spent much of their time at their home in Maine. Their cremated remains are on Mount Desert Island, Maine.

BIBLIOGRAPHY

Galey, Mathieu (1980). *Marguerite Yourcenar: With Open Eyes.* Boston: Beacon Press.

HANNAH GLUCKSTEIN AND NESTER OBERMER

We are not an affair are we, we are husband and wife.

Gluck to Nesta
(Souhami, 1988, p. 126)

Hannah Gluckstein (1895-January 10, 1978), British painter. Gluck (as most people called her) was born into a wealthy Jewish family whose fortune came from a catering company. She despised their money yet could not live without it, and was depressed much of her life. She was opposed to religion, usually cross-dressed, and was a bit of a rebel. Her colorful portraits and still lifes were highly acclaimed in the 1930s and 1940s, and again in the 1970s.

Nester Obermer (née Ella Ernestine Sawyer, 1894-1985), British broadcaster and writer under the pen name Nesta Sawyer. Nesta (as she was known) married Seymour, thirty years her senior, who accepted his wife's lesbianism. Gluck and Nesta's extant love letters exhibit little modesty. Gluck and Nesta married each other on May 25, 1936, and exchanged rings of commitment. Their marriage ended in 1944, and Gluck became lovers with Edith Shackleton Heald. Gluck's ashes were scattered in her studio garden.

BIBLIOGRAPHY

Souhami, Diana (1988). *Gluck: Her Biography.* London: Pandora Press.

ANGELINA WELD GRIMKÉ AND MAMIE BURRILL

Angelina Weld Grimké (February 27, 1880-June 10, 1958), American poet, schoolteacher. Grimké was from a prominent biracial Bostonian family descended from Southern slaves and slaveowners. She was a poet of the Harlem Renaissance and also wrote a feminist play, *Rachel* (1919). Grimké had no children, never married, and was reported as melancholy.

She was unabashedly in love with Mamie Burrill. Their relationship lasted seven years. In a letter to Burrill (October 27, 1896), Grimké wrote:

Oh Mamie if you only knew how my heart beats when I think of you and yearns and pants to gaze, if only for one second upon your lovely face.

In the same letter she asks Burrill to be her "wife." She signs the letter, "Your passionate lover."

Angelina Weld Grimké

ALBERTA HUNTER AND LOTTIE TYLER

Alberta Hunter (April 1, 1895-October 17, 1984), American singer, composer, nurse. Considered one of the greatest blues singers in American history, Hunter's long life took many unexpected turns. Her first lover was Carrie Mae Ward, whom she met in Chicago. Hunter met William Saxby Townsend in 1919 and married him two days later. They divorced after two months. Hunter then met in New York the love of her life, Lottie Tyler. The greatest significant other in Hunter's life was chorus line dancer Harry Watkins, who was her best friend for sixty years. Hunter, Tyler, and Watkins traveled to Europe (1928), where Hunter played "Queenie" in *Showboat* opposite Paul Robeson. Tyler fell in love with another woman, left Hunter in Europe, and returned to the States.

Alberta Hunter

Hunter was the first African-American woman entertainer for the United Service Organizations (1952). In 1956, Hunter quit her career as an entertainer to become a nurse in New York City. Later, she was forced into retirement from nursing because of her age. She revived her inner diva and sang at Carnegie Hall (1978) and the White House (1979). Her ashes are buried at Ferncliff Cemetery in Hartsdale, New York.

COUNTEE CULLEN AND HAROLD JACKMAN

The night whose sable breast relieves the stark
White stars is no less lovely, being dark;
And there are buds that cannot bloom at all
In light, but crumple, piteous, and fall;
So in the dark we hide the heart that bleeds,
And wait, and tend our agonizing seeds.

Countee Cullen
(Cullen, 1927, p. 184)

Countee Cullen (May 30, 1903-January 9, 1946), American poet, editor. A native of Harlem, Countee Cullen graduated from New York University (1925) Phi Beta Kappa, and with an MA from Harvard (1926). Cullen was a poet of conventional technique, modeling his works after John Keats. He wrote about contemporary black-American life during the Harlem Renaissance. His works include: *Color* (1925), *Copper Sun* (1927), *The Ballad of the Brown Girl* (1927), and *On These I Stand* (1947). Cullen also edited *Caroling Dusk: An Anthology of Verse by Negro Poets* (1927). Cullen also taught French in Harlem, his most notable student being **James Baldwin.**

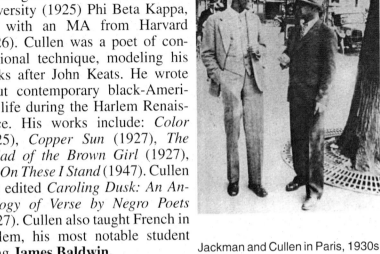

Jackman and Cullen in Paris, 1930s

The few opportunities for black-American poets to get published at that time were greatly diminished if one came out. Cullen hid his homosexuality. He married Yolande Du Bois (1928), daughter of W. E. B. Du Bois. After only two months of marriage, Cullen eloped to Europe with his best man and lover, Harold Jackman (August 18, 1901-1961), British-American educator and philanthropist. Jackman was an inspiration to many black-Americans as a teacher, and was a celebrated model for artists and photographers. Jackman was co-founder of the Harlem Experimental Theater and established the Countee Cullen Memorial Collection in Atlanta.

Cullen later married again (1940) while he was involved with another man.

BIBLIOGRAPHY

Cullen, Countee (ed.) 1927. *Caroling Dusk: An Anthology of Verse by Negro Poets.* New York: Harper & Brothers Publishers.
Ebony, August 19, 1971.

JAMES WHALE AND DAVID LEWIS

James Whale

James Whale (July 22, 1899-May 29, 1957), British-American movie director. As a prisoner of war in World War I, Whale began his career in entertainment by acting for his fellow prisoners. After the war, Whale joined stage productions as an actor, then as set designer, and finally as director. He moved to Hollywood (1930) when he got an offer to put his stage production, *Journey's End,* into film. In Whale's short career he directed twenty films, most notably his four horror films, *Frankenstein* (1931), *The Old Dark House* (1932), *The Invisible Man* (1933), *The Bride of Frankenstein* (1935), and his musical, *Show Boat* (1936). Discrepancy exists as to whether Whale's career ended (1941) so that he could "retire" and spend his time painting, or whether he was blacklisted for being openly gay.

David Lewis (né Levy, December 14, 1903-March 13, 1987), American movie producer. Lewis is responsible for contributing to the production of eighteen films, notably *Camille* (1936), *Dark Victory* (1939), and *The Other Love* (1947). Lewis worked closely with many stars, notably Bette Davis, Spencer Tracy, Jean Harlow, **Greta Garbo,** Elizabeth Taylor, and Ronald Reagan.

Lewis and Whale met in New York City (1929). They lived together for twenty-three years until Whale went to Europe for a year, returning (1953) with an additional lover, Pierre Foegel. Whale suggested to Lewis a ménage à trois in their Pacific Palisades home. But Lewis was not interested in an overlapping relationship, and moved out, living most of the rest of his twenty-five years as a recluse in a one-room apartment in West Hollywood. Whale added to their Amalfi Drive home a swimming pool, even though he could not swim. He wrote a suicide note to Lewis, and fully clothed, dove into the shallow end, smashing his skull and drowning.

Their ashes are inurned across from each other in the mausoleum at Forest Lawn Memorial Park, Glendale, California.

BIBLIOGRAPHY

Barnhill, Mark, "Mystery Lingers in Filmmaker's Death." *Daily News*, Los Angeles, April 12, 1987.

Curtis, James (1982). *James Whale*. London: The Scarecrow Press.

GRETA GARBO AND MERCEDES DE ACOSTA

Greta Garbo (née Gustafsson, September 18, 1905—April 15, 1990), Swedish-American movie star. Garbo's classic beauty and—at the advent of "talkies"—her husky and alluring voice made her the symbol of chic to Western women, her trousers and hats casting an air of assured sexuality. Because she often played tragic heroines—such as in *Anna Christie* (1930), *Anna Karenina* (1935), and *Camille* (1936)—when Garbo starred in *Ninotchka* (1939) the newspaper headlines read, "GARBO LAUGHS." She had a terrible fear of the press and the public, and in her attempts to avoid them, she was relentlessly pursued. Garbo retired in her prime (1941), living another half-century in seclusion. Garbo has a star in her honor on Hollywood's Walk of Fame.

Mercedes de Acosta (March 1, 1893-May 9, 1968), American screenwriter, mystic, sybarite. Born into a strict Catholic family of wealthy Spanish immigrants, de Acosta was rebellious, fun-loving, and outrageous. She was an ardent vegetarian who converted Garbo and many others. She was a psychic who practiced yoga, and was a devotee of Bhagavan Ramana Maharishi. She had an exotic and passion-filled life, seducing famous women the world over (including **Marlene Dietrich, Alla**

Mercedes de Acosta and Greta Garbo flee the paparazzi on Hollywood Boulevard, 1931

Nazimova, Isadora Duncan, Tallulah Bankhead, Pola Negri, and **Natalie Barney**), as she notes in her autobiography, *Here Lies the Heart* (1960).

Garbo never forgave de Acosta for that betrayal of confidence, and they remained estranged to death. De Acosta was a difficult, pushy person who died alienated from almost every one of her former friends; she died lonely, broke, and without the glamour she was so known for. She did not hide her lesbianism; Garbo hid everything. Whether or not these two dear friends—who spent six weeks together, alone in a log cabin on an uninhabited island—were sexually involved, we may never know for sure.

Garbo's ashes are buried at Skogskyrkogården Cemetery, Stockholm, Sweden. De Acosta is buried at Trinity Cemetery in New York City.

BIBLIOGRAPHY

de Acosta, Mercedes (1960). *Here Lies the Heart.* New York: Reynal & Company.
Gronowicz, Antoni (1990). *Garbo: Her Story.* New York: Viking.
Vickers, Hugo (1994). *Loving Garbo: The Story of Greta Garbo, Cecil Beaton, and Mercedes de Acosta.* New York: Random House.

CARY GRANT AND RANDOLPH SCOTT

I pretended to be somebody I wanted to be and I finally became that person. Or he became me. Or we met at some point. It's a relationship.

Cary Grant

Cary Grant and Randolph Scott were not gay. Or as **Paul Monette** used to say, "not gay enough." Cary Grant (né Archibald Alexander Leach, January 18, 1904-November 29, 1986), British-American

Randolph Scott and Cary Grant at home in the pool

movie star. George Randolph Crane Scott (January 23, 1898-March 2, 1987), American movie star. At age seventy-six, Cary Grant sued heterosexual actor Chevy Chase for $10 million for implying on television that Grant was gay. But when actress **Marlene Dietrich** had said (1966) Grant was a homosexual, Grant took no action. Grant and Scott always denied being homosexual.

Grant and Scott were considered two of the most handsome leading men of Hollywood in the 1930s. Scott was best known for being the rugged macho star of blockbuster Hollywood Westerns. Grant made seventy-two films and was given a special Oscar (1970). When Grant immigrated to New York, his first roommate was a female impersonator. His second roommate in Greenwich Village was an openly gay costume designer. Grant became a U.S. citizen (1942) as part of his war efforts. It was reported that he was arrested in Los Angeles for having sex with a young man in a public toilet but was never charged.

Grant and Scott met in the early 1930s through closeted homosexual millionaire Howard Hughes. Scott and Grant lived together in a small Hollywood bungalow until the studios insisted that they live apart. But they were inseparable. Perhaps poet **Walt Whitman** would have referred to their manly comradeship as "adhesive love." Within months they were back living together again. They often appeared in public, sans female companions, much to the chagrin of studio executives. Again they were split up, and again they moved back in with each other. Scott was married twice with two adopted children, and Grant was married five times, producing one daughter. Upon his death, Scott's estate was estimated at $50-100 million. He was interred at Elmwood Cemetery in Charlotte, North Carolina. The only film that Grant and Scott starred in together was *Hot Saturday* (1932).

Cary Grant and Randolph Scott sharing a musical moment in their kitchen

MARLENE DIETRICH AND CLAUDETTE COLBERT

Marlene Dietrich (née Marie Magdalene, December 27, 1901-May 6, 1992) German-American stage and film actress and singer. Her femme fatale Lola in *The Blue Angel* (1930) launched a long-celebrated and prolific career for Miss Dietrich. Notable films include *Shanghai Express* (1932), *Destry Rides Again* (1939), *Foreign Affair* (1948), *Witness for the Prosecution* (1957), and *Judgment at Nuremberg* (1961).

Marlene Dietrich and Claudette Colbert, June 1935

Lily Claudette Colbert (née Chauchoin, September 13, 1903-July 30, 1996), French-American stage and film actress. Notable of Colbert's sixty-four films are *It Happened One Night* (1934, Academy Award: Best Actress), *Private Worlds* (1935), *Since You Went Away* (1944), and *Parrish* (1961). Claudette Colbert had a bad marriage (1928-1935) with actor/director Norman Foster, and a good marriage (1935-1968) with her doctor Joel Pressman.

Dietrich was openly bisexual, having many lovers of both genders. We are uncertain of the passionate intensities between Dietrich and Colbert, but I doubt if either would be ashamed of whatever their relationship was. Here, truly, a picture is worth a thousand words.

BIBLIOGRAPHY

Bach, Steven (1992). *Marlene Dietrich: Life and Legend.* New York: Morrow.
"Hollywood Legend Claudette Colbert Dies." *Los Angeles Times,* July 31, 1996.
Thomas, Kevin, "Claudette Colbert Faced Life with Resilient Style." *Los Angeles Times,* August 2, 1996.

LAURENCE OLIVIER AND DANNY KAYE

Sir Laurence Kerr Olivier (May 22, 1907-July 11, 1989), British-American movie star. Olivier's long and illustrious career garnered many accolades, most notably a special Academy Award for his film *Henry V* (1944), which he directed, produced, and starred in; the Oscar for best actor in *Hamlet* (1948); and a third Oscar (1979) for lifetime achievement. Olivier was knighted (1947) and made a peer of the realm (1970), where he acquired a seat in the House of Lords, the first actor ever to have achieved this honor. Olivier was married three times: to lesbian actress Jill Esmond (1930-1940), and to heterosexual actresses Vivien Leigh (1940-1960), and Joan Plowright (1961-1989).

Danny Kaye (center) performs with Sir Laurence Olivier (right) at the London Palladium, June 22, 1955

Danny Kaye (né David Daniel Kaminsky, January 18, 1913-March 3, 1987), American movie star. Kaye was mostly known as a comedian whose career soared in the 1940s and early 1950s. He was presented a special Academy Award (1954) for his unique talents and service to the Academy and to the American people. His popularity waned in the late 1950s as he began focusing more of his time and energy into UNICEF. Kaye was married (1940) to writer Sylvia Fine.

Olivier and Kaye met at a Hollywood party in 1940; it is alleged that they had a ten-year sexual relationship during the 1950s. One story states that on March 13, 1953, Olivier returned from Italy and arrived at Idlewild Airport, New York. A uniformed customs officer inspected Olivier's passport and, in a thick accent informed him that a strip search would be necessary. The two men went into a cubicle and Olivier submitted to this complete body search. The officer then stepped back and removed his dark wig and latex mask; before the naked Olivier was prankster Danny Kaye. The story continues that before moving on to Los Angeles, they spent the night together at the St. Regis Hotel.

BIBLIOGRAPHY

Spotto, Donald (1991). *Laurence Olivier: A Biography.* London: HarperCollins.

WILLIAM HAINES AND JIMMIE SHIELDS

Too long forgotten is the beautiful romance of a legendary Hollywood couple. So notable are they, in fact, that their dear friend Joan Crawford once said of them, "Billy and Jimmie are the happiest married couple in Hollywood."

William Haines (January 1, 1900-December 26, 1973), American movie star, interior decorator. Billy Haines was an all-American gay-boy-next-door from Virginia who had manners, wit, style, and luck. He was "discovered" in New York, brought to Hollywood, soon fell

Jimmie Shields and husband Billy Haines host a party for friend Joan Crawford and her fourth husband Alfred Steele, 1955

into being a leading silent film star (1920s), and is now immortalized on Hollywood's Walk of Fame. Haines survived the transition to talkies while living an openly gay life with his lover, James Shields, (March 24, 1905-March 5, 1974), American interior decorator. But after the stock market crash, early in the 1930s, new censorship codes and Catholic mandates were imposed in Hollywood. Heterosexual Jewish studio mogul Louis B. Mayer said to his leading star William Haines, "You're either to give up that boyfriend of yours, or I'll cancel your contract" (Mann, 1998, p. 212). Haines made a lifestyle choice, giving up his celebrated career in Hollywood to spend nearly fifty years in legendary love.

After Billy and Jimmie and some friends were gay-bashed by white supremacists near Manhattan Beach (1936), the headlines outed them as homosexuals. They were dropped from most Hollywood guest lists. But some remained loyal, notably Crawford and gay American director George Cukor.

Haines and Shields started an interior decorating business to the stars, executives, and sybarites of Los Angeles. This second career was more profitable with less hassle. In an interview with *The New York Times* (1949), when asked if he missed his old stardom, Haines answered, "I'm content with my work. It's clean, no mascara on the face" (Goodman, 1949). For a twenty-fifth anniversary party for Haines and Shields, Haines sent an invitation to former boss L. B. Mayer and wrote on it, "And you said it wouldn't last." It lasted yet another quarter of a century. Their life and love got better as they aged.

Haines died of cancer in Santa Monica at age seventy-three. Not one obituary in his files at the Academy Library in Beverly Hills mentions his surviving lover. In his suicide note barely three months later, Jimmie Shields wrote, "It's no good without Billy."

BIBLIOGRAPHY

Goodman, Ezra, "Ringing Up the Curtain on William Haines." *The New York Times*, June 8, 1949.

Mann, William, personal communication, September 5, 1995, 1:00 p.m.

Mann, William J. (1998). *Wisecracker: The Life and Times of William Haines, Hollywood's First Openly Gay Star*. New York: Viking.

HANS HENNY JAHNN AND GOTTLIEB HARMS

Hans Henny Jahnn (1894-November 29, 1959) and Gottlieb Harms (c. 1893-February 1931), German writers, artists, utopians. All of Jahnn's eleven novels depict male homosexual love as a central theme. His diaries speak of his life with and love for Harms. Together they purchased a piece of farmland south of Hamburg and founded a gay male utopian community called Ugrino Commune. Ugrino was an anti-Christian haven for bohemian artists. Jahnn designed the buildings.

Jahnn and Harms married (1926) sisters Ellinor and Monna Philips. Jahnn fathered a daughter (1929). Jahnn and Harms are buried together.

MARGARET ANDERSON AND JANE HEAP

It was the poet, the artist, who discovered love, created the lover, made sex everything that it is beyond a function.

Jane Heap

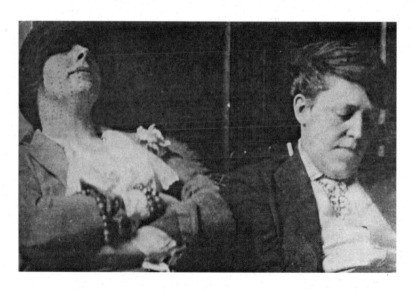

Margaret Anderson and Jane Heap, early 1920s

Margaret Caroline Anderson (November 24, 1886-October 18, 1973), American editor, writer. As an accomplished pianist and aspiring writer, Anderson left home and moved to Chicago to be a part of the bohemian literary community. After tedious book review jobs, Anderson founded the highly esteemed literary journal *The Little Review* (March 1914), publishing the poetry of **Amy Lowell, H.D.**, and **Gertrude Stein,** and essays of anarchism by **Emma Goldman,** the latter of which led to the loss of Anderson's major financial backer.

Jane Heap (1887-1964), American painter. Heap joined Anderson as lover (1916) and *The Little Review* as an art director, launching the magazine into wider circles and greater prominence. They moved their operations to New York (1917) and were brought to trial on obscenity charges (1920). In *The Little Review,* Anderson and Heap were not afraid to publish openly lesbian material and politically challenging ideology. The publication gave voice to unpublished artists (notably James Joyce) and previously unseen styles of writing. At the apex of collaboration between Heap and Anderson, *The Little Review* securely holds title to making significant contributions to the history of modern literature.

The couple split up when Anderson moved to Paris (1923) and turned the editorship over to Heap, but they remained lifelong friends and business partners. Heap gradually changed *The Little Review* to be less literary and include more art, specifically of the Dada and Surrealist movements. Heap opened a gallery on lower Fifth Avenue, and organized the International Theatre Exposition (1926) and the Machine Age Exposition (1927). Anderson adopted her terminally ill sister's children, with Heap as a legal partner in the adoption. It was Heap who assumed the responsibility for providing care and education for them.

In Paris, Anderson fell in love with French singer Georgette Leblanc. Her rekindled interest as a pianist was accompanied by the song of her new lover. They lived together until Leblanc's death (1941). Anderson then moved back to the States where she became lovers with Dorothy Caruso (widow of opera singer Enrico Caruso) for thirteen years. Margaret Anderson is buried in Notre Dame des Anges Cemetery next to Georgette Leblanc. Jane Heap committed suicide.

BIBLIOGRAPHY

Anderson, Margaret (1951). *The Fiery Fountains.* New York: Horizon Press.

J. EDGAR HOOVER AND CLYDE TOLSON

Words are mere man-given symbols for thoughts and feelings, and they are grossly insufficient to express the thoughts in my mind and the feelings in my heart that I have for you.

J. Edgar Hoover to Clyde Tolson (1943)
(Summers, 1993, p. 76)

John Edgar Hoover (January 1, 1895-May 2, 1972), founder of the Federal Bureau of Investigation (FBI). Clyde Anderson Tolson (May 22, 1900-April 14, 1975), associate director of the FBI. In this author's opinion, Hoover and Tolson are two of the most insidious homosexual homophobes in history. Hoover is most noted for creating the FBI and for overseeing it for more than forty years. As much as

A smirking J. Edgar Hoover with Clyde Tolson on the boardwalk at Atlantic City, NJ, September 8, 1938

we can give credit to Hoover for fighting crime in America (for example, he instituted fingerprint technology), we can now also confirm his willing participation in organized crime and treason. He worked hand-in-hand to help build the (Italian) American Mafia and knew well in advance of the possibility of the attacks on Pearl Harbor. Hoover maintained voluminous files of illegally obtained materials on the private and sexual lives of famous Americans. He made a career of ruining innocent people's lives, notably Ethel Rosenberg. FBI headquarters in Washington, DC, are located in the still-named J. Edgar Hoover Building.

Noted American sexologist Dr. John Money has suggested that there be named the "J. Edgar Hoover Syndrome" to describe those who, in order to manage the anxiety created by conflict over their own sexual identity, mask their own sexualities by compulsively obsessing about the sexualities of other extraordinary people. Money observed:

> Hoover's whole life was one of haunting and hounding people over their sexuality, brutalizing them one way or another because of it. He took on the role of being the paragon, keeping the country morally clean, yet hid his own sexual side. His terrible thing was that he needed constantly to destroy other people in order to maintain himself. Many people like that break down and end up needing medical help. Hoover managed to live with his conflict—by making others pay the price. (Summers, 1993, pp. 78-79)

Hoover suffered from many psychological disorders. He was a compulsive hand washer and a compulsive gambler whose racetrack habit was covered by the Mafia. Hoover and Tolson ate dinner together five nights a week for forty years at Harvey's Restaurant on Connecticut Avenue. Although we don't know a lot about their sexualities, they certainly were two strange guys. It is reported that Hoover was a transvestite who liked to be manipulated by rubber-gloved male hustlers while being read to from the Bible. Some might say that the fact that such a cruel, hateful, bigoted, straight-acting gay white man, afflicted by so many serious psychological and sexual disorders, was able to somehow find another straight-acting gay white man to be his colleague, friend, and lover for forty-four years is nothing short of a miracle.

As they both requested at their deaths, they are buried within yards of each other at the Congressional Cemetery. Truman Capote once referred to J. Edgar Hoover as "that killer fruit."

BIBLIOGRAPHY

Gentry, Curt (1991). *J. Edgar Hoover: The Man and the Secrets*. New York: Plume.
Summers, Anthony (1993). *Official and Confidential: The Secret Life of J. Edgar Hoover*. New York: G.P. Putnam's Sons.

J. C. LEYENDECKER AND CHARLES BEACH

Joseph Christian Leyendecker (March 23, 1874-July 25, 1951), German-American commercial artist. Born in Montabour, Germany, of Dutch parentage, raised in Chicago, and educated in Paris, Leyendecker was one of the world's most celebrated painters of advertisement campaigns. The young Norman Rockwell was so inspired by Leyendecker that he would go to the train platform daily to watch the famous artist arrive from his commute to be met by his limousine.

At age seventeen, J.C. Leyendecker had already begun a contract illustrating the Bible. Among his many lucrative contracts were Ivory Soap (1900), Kellogg's Corn Flakes (1912), periodic magazine covers for *The Saturday Evening Post* and *Colliers,* and war posters for the U.S. Navy (1917-1919). But his most famous campaign was for the shirt company Arrow Collar Man (1905-1930). Leyendecker's sexy blond model for the Arrow Collar Man was his lover, Charles Beach (1886-1952), Canadian-American model, business manager. Women across America fell instantly in love with this new supermodel. In one month, Beach received 17,000 fan letters, more than a few with proposals of marriage. The art of J.C. Leyendecker is pumping with homoeroticism, archetypically like an early technicolor Tom of Finland.

Beach and Leyendecker met in 1901 and were together for fifty years. Beach managed all of Leyendecker's affairs and received a percentage of the royalties. Beach also ran the mansion that they built together on Mt. Tom Road in New Rochelle, New York. Leyendecker died from a heart attack and left his estate equally to his sister, Augusta, and to Beach. Beach died soon after of alcoholism.

BIBLIOGRAPHY

The Advocate, January 28, 1976, p. 43.
J.C. Leyendecker Posterbook (1975). New York: Watson-Guptill Publications.
Schau, Michael (1974). *J.C. Leyendecker.* New York: Watson-Guptill Publications.

NATHAN LEOPOLD AND RICHARD LOEB

I thought so much of the guy that I was willing to do anything—
even murder—if he wanted it bad enough.

Leopold, about Loeb

Nathan "Babe" Leopold Jr. (November 19, 1904-August 31, 1971)
and Richard "Dickie" Loeb (June 11, 1905-January 28, 1936), American murderers. In what was often referred to as "The Crime of the
Century," on May 21, 1924, Leopold, nineteen, and Loeb, eighteen,
randomly murdered Bobby Franks, fourteen, simply for "the thrill."

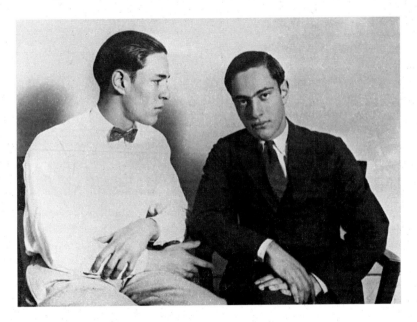

Nathan Leopold and Richard Loeb

Both murderers were highly intelligent sons of wealthy Chicagoan Jews. At eighteen, Leopold was the youngest-ever graduate from the University of Chicago. He spoke twenty-seven languages. His expensive horn-rimmed glasses with an unusual hinge were found at the murder scene; this assisted police in quickly apprehending the perpetrators. Legendary attorney Clarence Darrow defended Leopold and Loeb, claiming that their homosexuality was evidence of their insanity. Their trial led to a wave of anti-Semitism and homophobia in America. They were sentenced to life plus ninety-nine years.

Their sexual relationship was sadomasochistic, Loeb being the top and Leopold being the bottom. Three movies have been made about this notorious crime: *Rope* (1948), *Compulsion* (1959), and *Swoon* (1992). Loeb was killed in prison, slashed fifty-six times by an inmate claiming a homosexual panic defense. After his fourth application, Leopold was granted parole (February 1958) for his contributions to science and medicine. He lived the rest of his life in Puerto Rico, where he married widow Trudi Feldman (1961).

BIBLIOGRAPHY

"Freedom for Superman," *Time,* March 3, 1958, p. 14.
"Nathan Leopold, 66, Thrill Killer, Dies." *Los Angeles Times,* August 31, 1971.

ELISABETH MARBURY AND ELSIE DE WOLFE

Elisabeth Marbury (June 19, 1856-January 22, 1933), American theatrical agent and producer. Marbury was noted for her keen insight into literary and theatrical success. She established her reputation in Europe representing many illustrious clients, notably George Bernard Shaw and James Barrie *(Peter Pan),* and she published *The Ballad of Reading Gaol* for **Oscar Wilde** during his imprisonment. Upon returning to America, she brought credibility to Broadway, and was an early producer of homosexual composer Cole Porter. She was a large woman, weighing more than 200 pounds, and smoked four to five packs of cigarettes a day.

Elsie de Wolfe (December 20, 1865-July 12, 1950), American actress, interior decorator. Miss De Wolfe's brief successful career as an actor (by which she met Marbury in 1885) was supplanted by her more notable career as interior decorator to the rich and famous. With unlimited funds from turn-of-the-century industrialists, de Wolfe reintroduced classical thematic designs, making brilliant accommodations to modern inventions. De Wolfe professed anti-suffragist views, was a close friend of philanthropist Anne Morgan, and, with Wilbur Wright as pilot, was one of the first women to fly (1908). At age sixty (1926), de Wolfe married Sir Charles Mendl, acquiring her Ladyship and loosing her American citizenship. During World War II, Lady Mendl returned to the United States and regained her citizenship through a special act of Congress.

Marbury and de Wolfe lived together as lovers in New York City from 1887-1914.

RICHARD HALLIBURTON AND PAUL MOONEY

Richard Halliburton (1900-1939), American adventurer, writer, lecturer. Raised in Memphis, Tennessee, Halliburton eschewed the "commonplace quest for riches and respectability" (Hendrix, n.d.), and instead traveled the world in pursuit of the exotic, extraordinary, and forbidden. Halliburton swam the Hellespont strait and the Panama Canal; climbed the Matterhorn, Mt. Olympus, and Mt. Fujiyama; crossed the Alps by elephant in the tradition of Hannibal; and leapt seventy feet into the Mayan Well of Death at Chichén Itzá. His adventures—which took him to India, Arabia, and Africa—were supported by his syndicated travelogues that appeared regularly in periodicals, his six books, and his American lecture tours (during which, although he was financially solvent, he preferred to stay at YMCAs). Halliburton was a household name throughout the 1920s and 1930s, a symbol of manly courage in the face of unpredictable nature, and an exemplar of American compassion to people of all colors and all nations. He was a homosexual xenophile who quested for the international dear love of comrades.

In 1927, Halliburton hired a male secretary named Albert Shattuck. Shattuck lived, traveled, and worked with him for two years. As was his on-the-move pattern, Halliburton was predisposed to intense short-term affairs. Perhaps his most significant love relationship was with Paul Mooney (unknown-1939), American adventurer, writer. Mooney's father was an ethnologist with the Smithsonian Institute, hired to study the languages and traditions of Native Americans. Young Paul often traveled with his father, cultivating wanderlust and an appreciation for other cultures. Mooney had already established himself as a writer when he joined up with Halliburton to help him with his literary occupation, doing some of the writing that Halliburton is credited with. In 1937, Mooney and Halliburton were horseback riding high on a cliff overlooking South Laguna Beach when they stopped to watch the red ball of sunset. In this romantic moment they decided to build a home on that spot, which was known as Hangover House due to its juxtaposition on the cliff.

Halliburton and Mooney were crossing the Pacific Ocean, from Hong Kong to San Francisco, with about twelve companions on a Chinese junk when they were lost at sea, somewhere in the vicinity of Midway Island. Halliburton's father, executor of his estate, has removed all references to Paul Mooney from his son's correspondence and journals.

BIBLIOGRAPHY

Blankenship, Michael, "A Fellow Traveller;" *The Advocate,* July 18, 1989.
Hendrix, Kathleen (n.d.). "Richard Halliburton," *Los Angeles Times.*
Root, Jonathan (1965). *Halliburton: The Magnificent Myth.* New York: Coward-McCann, Inc.

MARINA TSVETAEVA AND SOPHIA PARNOK

My heart said at once: you are my love.

Marina Tsvetaeva to Sophia Parnok
(Feiler, 1994, p. 65)

Marina Ivanova Tsvetaeva (October 9, 1892-August 31, 1941), Russian poet. Tsvetaeva's was the tortured life of a poet; she was often on the run and in exile. Her grandfather was a priest, and against the wishes of her family, she married a Jew (Moscow, 1912) and had two children. In 1914, she met and fell in love, and had an intense and public affair with Sophia Parnok (1885-August 1933), Russian poet. Parnok was from a middle-class Jewish family and married (1907) for only a year and a half, supposedly for purposes of inheritance.

Sophia Parnok   Marina Tsvetaeva

Parnok then was comfortable with being out as a lesbian. She had many women lovers, notably Faina Ranevskaya and Olga Tsuberbiller. Parnok converted to Greek Orthodoxy and was prominent in the Moscow literary scene (1916). It was in this chic café society that these literati met. They were both famous in Russia, celebrated poets of the revolution, and known in literary circles throughout Europe.

Tsvetaeva was never comfortable with her own bisexuality or with lesbianism as a way of life. In 1934, she wrote "Letter to an Amazon" in response to a work by **Natalie Barney**: in it Tsvetaeva trashes Barney, Parnok, and lesbianism. Tsvetaeva felt trapped in her procreational family—her lifestyle choice—and was envious of lesbians who were happy and out. Parnok left Tsvetaeva, partly because Marina would not make a commitment. Parnok nevertheless kept a photo of her elusive lover next to her bed for the rest of her life.

After the revolution, under the tyranny of Stalin, the new Soviet regime was not tolerant of gays and lesbians, poets and artists, Jews and those who married them. Parnok and Tsvetaeva's works were silenced and banned. Tsvetaeva's children were sent to a gulag in Siberia and not released until the 1950s. It is only recently that their poetry is being rediscovered, along with evidence of a once-flowering queer Moscow community.

Parnok's last lover was physicist Nina Vedeneyeva. Parnok's untimely death was due to heart complications. Perhaps any amateur dream analyst could decipher Tsvetaeva's 1940 notebook entry (a year before she hanged herself):

> Then I saw in a dream S P, of whom I *never* think and whose death I didn't regret for a second—everything burnt out *clean then*—. In short, I saw her with her stupid woman friend and with her very naive poems. I left them—the friend and the poems—and went to some train compartment of third or even fourth class. (Feiler, 1994, p. 77)

BIBLIOGRAPHY

Feiler, Lily (1994). *Marina Tsvetaeva: The Double Beat of Heaven and Hell.* London: Duke University Press.
Proffer, Ellendea (1980). *Tsvetaeva: A Pictorial Biography.* Ardis.

BENJAMIN BRITTEN AND PETER PEARS

Lord

Sir Benjamin Britten (November 22, 1913-December 4, 1976), British composer. Sir Peter Neville Luard Pears (June 22, 1910-April

Peter Pears and Benjamin Britten, May 1976

3, 1986), British tenor. Britten and Pears shared forty-two years together in love, music, sex, art, and travel. Considered by some the most important composer of the twentieth century, Britten's prolific accomplishments include three pederasty-themed operas: *Peter Grimes* (1945), *The Turn of the Screw* (1954), and *Death in Venice* (1973). Pears' celebrated career often included premiering Britten's operas—the abovementioned plus *Billy Budd* and *Gloriana*—at such fabled houses as London's Covent Garden and New York's Metropolitan Opera.

They shared rooms with **W. H. Auden** and his lover **Chester Kallman** (1940) while collaborating on *Paul Bunyan* (1941). From Pears' diary and oral reports we know that Peter was "highly sexed and well endowed," unabashedly departing his company to follow a gentleman into the tearoom. "Britten played what used to be called a passive role" (Headington, 1992, p. 321).

Britten was knighted by Queen Elizabeth (1976), making him perhaps the first openly gay man awarded such honor. When he died, the customary spousal honors were extended to his lover, Peter Pears. They are buried together at Parish Church in Aldeburgh.

made a peer when dying

BIBLIOGRAPHY

Headington, Christopher (1992). *Peter Pears: A Biography*. London: Faber & Faber.

MARY RENAULT AND JULIE MULLARD

Julie and Mary moving to South Africa, 1948

Affairs may have trickled by, but this relationship of legendary love flourished for forty-eight years. Mary Renault (née Eileen Mary Challens, September 4, 1905-December 12, 1983), British-South African novelist. Julie Mullard (1912-August 2006), British-South African nurse, companion. They met as student nurses in England (1934), sneaking into each other's dormitory late at night. Mary once brought Julie a cup of hot milk and was

Julie and Mary at their home, Delos, on the beach at Camps Bay, Capetown

so silent in her entrance that she startled Julie. Julie knocked the sear-
ing beverage, seriously burning her chest. This episode began a half
century of their nursing and caring for each other.

Renault assumed her pen name with the publication of the first in a
series of lesbian-themed novels. An MGM Award (1947) of 37,000
pounds ($150,000) offered some independence from drudgery, and
so Mary and Julie decided to set sail for South Africa (1948), which
became their permanent home. They attained citizenship in 1950. On
the ship they met a gay male couple—both actors—setting a trend for
friendships that Renault and Mullard cultivated in their new country.
Mary was politically active with PEN International, and the Black
Sash protest marches against apartheid (1955). But undoubtedly
Renault's greatest contribution to the world was her series of historical novels depicting homoeroticism in ancient Greece, most notably:
The King Must Die (1958), *The Mask of Apollo* (1966), and *The Persian Boy* (1972). The commercial success of her books brought homosexuality in history out of the locked, back rooms of libraries and

into the homes of millions. She gave gay men of the 1960s a gift of classical entitlement to their blooming pride.

Although they only visited Greece twice, Julie and Mary's passion for the country remained constant. Mullard scattered Renault's ashes (1987) in a spot they'd both loved.

BIBLIOGRAPHY

Sweetman, David (1993). *Mary Renault: A Biography.* New York: Harcourt Brace.

GERTRUDE STEIN AND ALICE B. TOKLAS

In me meeney miney mo
You are my love and I tell you so

Stein to Toklas
(Souhami, 1991, p. 11)

From the day they met in 1907 Gertrude and Alice never traveled, entertained, or slept apart for the next thirty-eight years. Gertrude Stein (February 3, 1874-July 27, 1946), genius, poet, cultural mag-

net, and Alice Babette Toklas (April 30, 1877-March 7, 1967), devoted companion, culinary expert, secretary, needlepointer, had much in common by the time they met in their 30s. Both were born into moderately prosperous San Francisco area–families of first-generation European Jewish immigrants. Both had visited Europe as children, were well-educated, and lost their mothers when they were in their teens.

Their main residence was at 27 rue de Fleurus, in Paris, where their legendary salons were held. Many of the greatest artists in the

Gertrude Stein and Alice B. Toklas on the terrace at Bilignin, 1938

world, especially writers and painters, paid visits to the Stein and Toklas residence, a focal point of art and culture in Paris for four de-cades. Referring to many of the American expatriates who lived in Europe between the wars, Stein, in talking to Ernest Hemingway one day, coined the term, *the lost generation.* Stein and Toklas lived mod-estly on Stein's inheritance and occasional sales of her vast art collec-tion, which included many paintings by Picasso, Matisse, Cézanne, and other modern artists. In addition to their Parisian flat, they also rented a large home in the Rhône valley for fifteen years. They always employed help, had a succession of canine companions, and were quite attached to their automobiles, one of which was named Pris-cilla.

Toklas had a large cyst on her forehead, which is why she always wore bangs and often a hat. She was short with a big nose and a noto-rious mustache. She was a saint. She was reserved and always faded into the background, giving the spotlight to Gertrude. Alice kept the house, typed all of Gertrude's tricky syntax, was a celebrated chef, and navigated to Gertrude's piloting. Life was very difficult for Alice after Gertrude died of cancer. She refused to sell any of Gertrude's paintings, keeping the collection complete, and consequently lived a pauper's twilight. At age seventy-six, she was unable to pay her util-ity bills, and her heat was shut off. Alice was offered a book deal by a friend who secured her an advance. She locked herself away for three months to complete *The Alice B. Toklas Cookbook.* In it was a recipe for hashish brownies.

Stein and Toklas are buried together in Paris at the cemetery Père Lachaise. Alice had Gertrude's name inscribed boldly on the front of the tombstone (although some of the information is incorrect). And as an example of her meek and self-effacing way, visitors must walk around to the back of the stone to see that Alice had etched in small letters the name of Gertrude's humble, loving, and faithful compan-ion.

BIBLIOGRAPHY

Burns, Edward (ed.) (1973). *Staying on Alone: Letters of Alice B. Toklas.* New York: Liveright.
Souhami, Diana (1991). *Gertrude and Alice.* London: Pandora Press.

ALAN TURING AND CHRISTOPHER MORCOM

Alan Mathison Turing (June 23, 1912-June 7, 1954), British mathematician, hero, inventor, genius. Gloominess finally lifted for Alan Turing (1927) when he met Christopher C. Morcom (July 13, 1911-February 13, 1930), the true love of his life. Best buddies and scientific experimenters, Turing and Morcom were inseparable until Morcom's untimely death from an earlier infection of bovine tuberculosis. Morcom was an accomplished pianist and a better math student than Turing; a life of collaboration seemed imminent. It is said that Alan never recovered emotionally from Chris's death.

Alan Turing getting on the bus

Turing was educated at the University of Manchester and King's College, Cambridge, where he was awarded a Fellowship at age twenty-two. His paper "On Computable Numbers" (1936) laid the groundwork for developing contemporary computers, and he co-invented the first "Automatic Computing Engine" (1950).

During World War II, Turing was assigned to the Government Code and Cypher School, outside London, where he developed a machine that broke "Enigma," the German Nazis' most secret code. This provided the Allied forces with much-needed information, saving tens of thousands of lives. Some experts attribute the quantity of information procured through Turing's efforts as the coup de grâce to the Nazis and World War II. Turing was awarded Officer of the British Empire (1946) and Fellow of the Royal Society (1951).

Turing, a marathon runner and atheist, was arrested in 1952 and convicted of "gross indecencies" under an 1885 law. He was openly homosexual in a time when American McCarthyism was being exported, proclaiming gays and lesbians as security risks. Turing was sentenced to the cure of the week: injections of estrogen. He developed female-like breasts and erectile disorder, and became despondent. Turing died from eating an apple soaked in cyanide. It is alleged that he committed suicide. No suicide note was found.

BIBLIOGRAPHY

Hodges, Andrew (1983). *Alan Turing: The Enigma.* New York: Simon & Schuster.

DOROTHY THOMPSON AND CHRISTA WINSLOE

. . . an incredible feeling of sisterhood.

Dorothy Thompson
(Sanders, 1973, p. 180)

They first met in 1926 when Christa Winsloe's name was still Baroness Hatvany of Budapest. But it wasn't until their next meeting, in Christmas 1932, that these ladies got serious about each other. Mrs. Lewis (Dorothy Thompson), in her green pajamas, answered the

Dorothy Thompson in Budapest, age 28   Christa Winsloe

knock at her door at 7 a.m. Glad to see the baroness, she went to shake hands, but instead they kissed. Later that day her diary entry reads:

> [I]mmediately I felt the strange, soft feeling—curious—of being at home, and at rest; an enveloping warmth and sweetness like a drowsy bath. (Sanders, 1973, p. 178)

And a few days later:

> What in God's name does one call this sensibility if it be not love? (p. 180)

Dorothy Thompson (July 9, 1893-January 30, 1961), American journalist. Attending Syracuse University (1912), Thompson became active in the women's suffrage movement, which determined her life of political involvement. She wrote for many newspapers and magazines across the country for more than forty years, including the *New York Evening Post, New York Herald Tribune, Foreign Affairs, Ladies' Home Journal,* and *Atlantic Monthly.* She was a regular ABC radio commentator, and was considered by some as the second most important female American voice after **Eleanor Roosevelt.** Perhaps her biggest career mistake was when she reported in her interview with Adolf Hitler (*Cosmopolitan,* 1931) that he was of "startling insignificance." But by 1933, Thompson was one of America's most powerful editorial voices opposing Hitler and demanding U.S. intervention. In July 1934, she was officially expelled from Germany.

Thompson had three marriages, the first in 1922 to a Hungarian Jew, Josef Bard. The second (1928) was to writer Sinclair Lewis, by whom she bore a son. It was with Lewis that she purchased the 300-acre Twin Farms estate in Vermont, sanctuary for many European refugees. Thompson's third husband (1943) was Maxim Kopf.

Christa Winsloe (December 23, 1888-June 10, 1944), German author, sculptor. Winsloe left her homosexual Hungarian husband, the Baron of Hatvany, and her privileged life to be an outspoken international lesbian. Winsloe's lesbian novel *Mädchen in Uniform* (English translation, 1932) was made into a movie (1931). Winsloe loudly advocated against German National-Socialism and its inherent bigotry and facilitated the escape of countless Jews. Her political savvy, sense of humor, and compassion for humanity matched that of Thompson's.

After a long diary entry about having delicious unexpected sex with her husband, Thompson wrote at the end: "I have been very, very happy. And all the time, every moment, I have thought of Christa" (Sanders, 1973, p. 181).

Their relationship peaked during Thompson's marriage to Lewis. Winsloe moved to Hollywood briefly but was financially unsuccessful, moving finally to France (1935). When the Germans confiscated Winsloe's assets, Thompson supported her girlfriend until the end. While residing in Cluny, Saône-et-Loire, Winsloe and her Swiss lover, writer Simone Gentet, were murdered, apparently by either a common criminal or by Nazi secret service agents.

Dorothy Thompson, a Zionist since 1920, went to Palestine after the war (1945). Concerned about the inevitable immigration of hundreds of thousands of Jews, the displacement of Palestinians, and finally the bombing of the King David Hotel by Zionist terrorists (which killed ninety-one people), Thompson reversed her position on a Jewish state, costing her dearly in America. By 1950 she shifted her political focus to world disarmament. She died of a heart attack in Lisbon, Portugal.

If she had lived into the 1970s, one could speculate that Dorothy Thompson would have—at the least—self-identified as a *political lesbian.* Thompson was evidently a happy, predominantly heterosexual woman. And Christa Winsloe may have been her brief and only *amorada lesbiana.* But to be sure, Winsloe—a story yet recovered—was the love that lit up and sparkled in Dorothy Thompson "an incredible feeling of sisterhood."

BIBLIOGRAPHY

Sanders, Marion K. (1973). *Dorothy Thompson: A Legend in Her Time.* New York: Avon.

JOE ORTON AND KENNETH HALLIWELL

John Kingsley Orton (January 1, 1933-August 9, 1967), British writer. Kenneth Leith Halliwell (June 23, 1926-August 9, 1967), British collaborator. Orton and Halliwell met as students at the Royal Academy of Dramatic Arts (1951) and remained together for the next fifteen years. Orton was a celebrated playwright and iconoclast known for his farcical comedies and their cynical humor. Halliwell helped write, edit, and produce these plays but never received public acknowledgment for his efforts.

As a child, Halliwell witnessed his mother get stung by a wasp and die moments later. He also discovered his dead father, who had committed suicide by putting his head in a gas oven. Halliwell and Orton spent six months in jail (1962) for defacing library books. Orton was notorious for frequenting public toilets for sexual interactions. Halliwell was jealous of Orton's notoriety and promiscuity. Halliwell bludgeoned his lover to death with nine hammer blows to the skull. He then swallowed twenty-two Nembutals with a grapefruit juice chaser and died within thirty seconds.

BIBLIOGRAPHY

Lahr, John (1978). *Prick Up Your Ears*. New York: Avon.

RUDI GERNREICH AND ORESTE PUCCIANI

Rudolph Gernreich (August 8, 1922-April 21, 1985), Austrian-American fashion designer. Gernreich received fourteen Coty American Fashion Critics Awards and the cover of *Time* magazine (1967) during his celebrated career. He is attributed with the invention of miniskirts, the no-bra bra, the concept of "unisex," and the topless bathing suit. Gernreich was a founding member of the Los Angeles Mattachine Society (1950-1953), and had an affair with activist faerie Harry Hay.

Oreste Francesco Pucciani (April 7, 1916-April 28, 1999), American educator, translator. Pucciani graduated Western Reserve University Phi Beta Kappa, and completed his PhD at Harvard in Romance Languages. His dissertation, "The Literary Reputation of **Walt Whitman** in France," was one of his several published works. Pucciani was a professor of French and existentialist philosophy at UCLA for thirty-one years. He was one of the first to translate Jean-Paul Sartre into English (1954), and was awarded the French Legion of Honor (1965).

Rudi was Oreste's third lover. Pucciani's second lover, bisexual French-American Jacques Faure, had an affair with **David Lewis** and then left Pucciani for an Italian woman. This freed Pucciani to be available for Gernreich, who tagged along to a cocktail party at Pucciani's Laurel Canyon, California, home. It was love at first sight for both of them, commitment immediately to follow. Their relationship remained sexually active and was always sexually non-exclusive. Pucciani and Gernreich were together for thirty-two years.

BIBLIOGRAPHY

Pucciani, Oreste, personal communication, September 26, 1996.

JACK KEROUAC AND NEAL CASSADY

Jack (né Jean-Louis Lebris de) Kerouac (March 12, 1922-October 21, 1969), and Neal Cassady (c. 1926-February 4, 1968), American writers, beatniks. When Kerouac knocked on the door to meet the notorious Neal Cassady, Cassady, in the nude, flung the door open. (Cassady, twenty, had just married his first wife Luanne, sixteen.) From that moment on, they were best friends and ludic lovers.

Kerouac is known as the "father of the beat generation." His rambling, personal, and authentically American prose often depicted a postwar American spirit of iconoclasm, and a journey for self-discovery through narcotics, jazz, and Eastern philosophies, notably *The Town and the City* (1950), *On the Road* (1957), *The Dharma Bums* (1958), *Desolation Angels* (1965), and *Pic* (1971). Kerouac was married to Edie Parker (1944-annulled

Neal Cassady and Jack Kerouac, c. 1952

1945), Joan Haverty (1950-divorced, one daughter), and Stella Sampas (1966). Cassady never achieved the literary notoriety that Kerouac did, and sometimes felt that he lived in his buddy's shadow. Cassady's second wife, with whom he shared most of his life, was Carolyn Robinson.

Cassady was a rebel without a cause, a car thief, a live wire, and the focus of most of Kerouac's novels. Their closest friends were gay male literati (many of whom claim to have had sexual interactions with either or both of them, often in drunken states), notably Allen Ginsburg, Peter Orlovsky, William S. Burroughs, Gregory Corso, and Gore Vidal. Whereas Cassady was a lady's man and developed a reputation as a conqueror of females, Kerouac garnered the opposite, with his fumbling attempts at coitus. Witnesses attest that the relationship between Kerouac and Cassady was at times sexual. Possibly from the first nude encounter of Cassady, Kerouac was envious of Cassady's sexual self-assuredness. It would not be preposterous to speculate that Cassady was bisexual and that Kerouac, struggling with Catholicism and a dominant mother, never came to terms with his gayness. It is alleged that Kerouac once entered a bar in New York and shouted that he had sucked Gore Vidal's cock.

Cassady took an overdose of Seconal and pulque (a strong Mexican drink) and died in San Miguel de Allende, Mexico. Kerouac turned into a political conservative and died of illness due to alcoholism at his mother's home in Florida.

BIBLIOGRAPHY

Cassady, Carolyn (1976). *Heart Beat: My life with Jack and Neal.* New York: Simon & Schuster.

Cassady, Carolyn (2007). *Off the Road: My Twenty Years with Cassady, Kerouac and Ginsberg.* London: Black Spring Press, Ltd.

Gifford, Barry and Lee, Lawrence (1978). *Jack's Book.* New York: St. Martin's Press.

HARVEY MILK AND JOE CAMPBELL

Harvey Bernard Milk (May 22, 1930-November 27, 1978), gay martyr, political activist, clown. From an assimilated Jewish-Ameri-

Harvey Milk and Joe Campbell, September 1956

can family, Harvey was athletic, a linebacker on his high school foot-ball team. After college graduation (1951), Harvey joined the U.S. Navy (1951-1955) and rose through the ranks rapidly. Milk said this was because he coached his ship's wrestling team to the champion-ships.

Joe Campbell (November 4, 1936-October 2, 2005) was raised in Chicago and New York. Not fitting in well, Joe was often beaten up by the other boys. Joe and Harvey met in July 1956 at Riis Park Beach in Queens. They were lovers for six years, the longest relationship ei-ther one ever had. Harvey taught high school math and history, coach-ing basketball after school, and enjoyed their middle-class domestic bliss. But whereas Harvey was more politically oriented, Joe was more bohemian. Harvey soon fatigued of the routine and wanted out. Joe was later dubbed the Sugar Plum Fairy by the Andy Warhol crowd who frequented Kelly's bar, a hustler workplace where Joe hung out. Campbell is the Sugar Plum Fairy that rocker Lou Reed is referring to in his hit song, "Walk on the Wild Side."

Both Milk and Campbell (separately) moved to San Francisco. Milk opened a camera store and became California's first openly gay elected official. He is famous for his enthusiasm, dedication to gay rights, and making of remarkable political alliances (such as that between the Teamsters and gay bars in the boycott of Coors beer). But Harvey was also known for his humor, for dressing up in his clown costume and hanging off of moving streetcars screaming, "I'm your elected supervisor!" His speeches often began with, "My name is Harvey Milk, and I'm here to recruit you."

San Francisco City Supervisor Harvey Milk was assassinated along with Mayor George Moscone in premeditated cold blood by homophobe Dan White, ex-supervisor, ex-police officer, Irish-Catholic potato vendor. The jury found White guilty of only two counts of voluntary manslaughter due to what is now infamously known as the Twinkie Defense. Milk had premonitions that he would be assassinated and left audio recordings with instructions should this happen.

Earlier, when Joe Campbell's lover (after Harvey) had broken up with him, Campbell fell into a coma as a result of attempted suicide. In the hospital, Harvey sat vigil next to Joe until he awoke. In the meantime Harvey had written a letter to Joe that ends with:

> Life is rotten—hard—bitter and so forth—but life is life and the best that we have—no one should take another's—no one should let another take his—people in worse situations than you have come back strong—have been against worse odds and won—only because they felt that somewhere there was some reason for living—they are not sure, but they had hope.

Love As Always, H.
(Shilts, 1982, p. 37)

BIBLIOGRAPHY

Shilts, Randy (1982). *The Mayor of Castro Street: The Life and Times of Harvey Milk*. New York: St. Martin's Press.

PAUL MONETTE AND ROGER HORWITZ

When we came together as lovers we knew precisely how happy we were. I only realized then that I'd never had someone to play with before.

Monette to Horwitz
(Monette, 1988, p. 13)

Paul Landry Monette (October 16, 1945-February 10, 1995), American writer, activist. Monette was a straight-A student, receiving full scholarship to his local Andover, Massachusetts, preparatory school, Phillips Academy, where he continued to get straight As. He graduated from Yale (1967) with a degree in English, where he was class poet. Monette subsequently received honorary doctorates from the

Paul Monette and Roger Horwitz at the monastery Monte Oliveto, Tuscany, 1983

State University of New York (SUNY) at Oswego (1992), Wesleyan University (1993), and City University of New York (1994). Monette's nineteen written works include poetry, fiction, novelizations, and memoir. *Becoming a Man: Half A Life Story* garnered Monette the National Book Award for Nonfiction (1992). Among his many other awards, Monette was the first American to receive France's prestigious MEDEC (1990) for Humanism in Medicine.

Roger David Horwitz (November 22, 1941-October 22, 1986), American bohemian, attorney. Horwitz grew up in Chicago and graduated from Harvard with a PhD in Comparative Literature (1972) and Law (1973). After several years in France, Horwitz returned to the States to begin practicing law. For a short while he had a radio show advocating for gay rights and marriage equality.

Monette and Horwitz met at a party in Boston (September 4, 1974), and moved to Los Angeles in November 1977. Together with Roger's half-brother Sheldon Andelson, Monette and Horwitz spent much of their time strategizing and organizing the gay community of Los Angeles. When Roger was diagnosed with AIDS, their focus shifted to AIDS activism, which is when Monette's literary work flourished. After Roger's death, Monette was lovers with Stephen Kolzak, and then Winston Wilde.

Before his death, Monette set up a charitable organization, The Monette-Horwitz Trust, which honors individuals and organizations who have made significant contributions to the eradication of homophobia.

Paul and Roger are buried together at Forest Lawn Cemetery, Hollywood Hills.

Paul—The most important thing to say is this: With you it's been the best—the best years and the most love.

Horwitz to Monette, 1980
(Monette, 1988, p. 326)

BIBLIOGRAPHY

Monette, Paul (1988). *Borrowed Time: An AIDS Memoir*. San Diego: Harcourt, Brace, Jovanovich, Publishers.

Glossary

abstinence: denial of the appetites: pleasure, alcohol, food, sex

agape: love of deity or holiness; altruistic love; love of nature

amitié amoureuse: romantic friendship

BCE: before the Common Era

beastiality: human/animal sex; interspecies sex; zoophilia

berdache: *See* TWO-SPIRIT

Boston marriage: late nineteenth-century term for two women in companionate love

celibacy: the taking of religious vows to not marry

chastity: state of being morally pure, and especially not engaging in unlawful sexual activity

chronophilia: the erotic love of age difference

companionate love: a constellation often with a domestic foundation; may be sexual or not

constellation: romantic relationship of two or more people

couple: a union of two people

entombed: placement of a corpse in a crypt of a wall

Eros: Greek demigod; love of beauty; sexual love

exotic love: *See* XENOPHILIA

fetishism: the deification, adoration, or love of an object or body part

fidelity: faithfulness, loyalty: conformity to truth, accuracy (does not imply sexuality)

Legacies of Love: A Heritage of Queer Bonding
© 2008 by The Haworth Press, Taylor & Francis Group. All rights reserved.
doi:10.1300/5890_09

gender: social identity constructed from anatomy, genitals, behavior, and dress

heterogendered couple: a union of one female and one male

heterosex: an interaction between male(s) and female(s) involving stimulation of genitals

homogamy: the tendency for selection of a spouse similar to oneself

homophilia: sexual love of the same gender

homosex: an interaction of two or more males or two or more females involving stimulation of their genitals

infatuation: a state of unreasoning short-lived passion or attraction: indicative of folly

interclass love: love of someone from a different socioeconomic status

intergenerational love: an interaction of two or more people with ten years or greater difference in age, or persons of perceived great difference (e.g., a fourteen-year-old and a twenty-one-year-old)

interred: in-ground burial of body or ashes of body

inurned: placement of cremated remains in a niche of a wall

*l'amour bleu***:** (French) gay male love

*l'amour fou***:** (French) the silly love, crazy love, *thea mania*

limerence: being infatuated with another human; uncontrolled passion

love: an intense affectionate concern or attachment

lover: a person of romantic interest

ludis: playful love of multiple partners without commitment

mania: craziness, obsessive love

mating: a series, or part of a series, of physical rituals culminating in sexual activity

ménage à trois*:* (French) household of three

monandry: having one male spouse

monogamy: having one female spouse; commonly used to indicate sexual exclusivity

né: original, former, or legal name (male)

née: original, former, or legal name (female)

overlapping love: a romantic interaction of two or more people where one or more partners acquire additional partners while primary partners retain loyalty

pair-bonding: heterosexual coupling for reproductive purposes

pederasty: sexual love of adolescents

pedophilia: sexual love of prepubescent children

philandering: engaging in love affairs frivolously, casually (Greek *philandros*: love of man)

philia: (Greek suffix) sexual love of

polyamory: having many lovers

polyandry: having many male spouses

polygamy: having many female spouses

pragma: practical (pragmatic) love

queer: deviation from the norm, especially in sexual orientation and/or gender identification

relationship: an interaction

roman à clef: (French) "novel with a key"; a real-life story told as fiction

romantic: the inclination to dream of love, heroism, or adventure

sexual exclusivity: an erotic boundary, usually of two people reserving sexual interactions for each other

spouse: domestic partner

storge: brotherly love, neighborly love

thea mania: (Greek) god-sent madness of love

two-spirit: general term attributed to gender-variant indigenous Americans

urolophilia: the sexual love of urine

utopian love: a relationship of four or more individuals who romantically pursue the quixotic goal of the perfect social, political and/or spiritual life, by living, working, and loving together

xenophilia: the sexual love of foreigners, strangers, or those who are different, especially those of different skin tones or those speaking foreign languages

zoophilia: sexual love of a human for an animal

Bibliography

Alyson, Sasha (ed.) (1993). *The Alyson Almanac: 1994-95 Edition*. Boston: Alyson Publications.

Babcock, Barbara (1986). *Daughters of the Desert: Women Anthropologists and the Native American Southwest*. Albuquerque: University of New Mexico Press.

Banner, Lois (1980). *Elizabeth Cady Stanton: A Radical for Women's Rights*. Boston: Little, Brown Co.

Barnard, Mary (1966). *Sappho: A New Translation*. Berkeley: University of California Press.

Bem, D. J. (2000). "Exotic Becomes Erotic: Interpreting the Biological Correlates of Sexual Orientation," *Archives of Sexual Behavior, 29,* 531-538.

Beurdeley, Cecile (1977). L'Amour Bleu; Evergreen: label of Benedickt Tasch Verlag GmbH, Koln, printed in Spain.

Chernow, Barbara A. and Vallasi, George A. (eds.) (1993). *The Columbia Encyclopedia: Fifth Edition*. The Columbia University Press, Houghton Mifflin Company.

Cowan, Thomas (1988). *Gay Men & Women Who Enriched the World*. Connecticut: Mulvey Books.

Cullen, Countee (ed.) (1927). *Caroling Dusk: An Anthology of Verse by Negro Poets*. New York: Harper & Brothers Publishers.

Duberman, Martin Bauml, Vincus, Martha and Chauncey, George, Jr. (1989). *Hidden from History: Reclaiming the Gay and Lesbian Past*. New York: New American Library, Penguin.

Dynes,Wayne R. (ed.) (1990). *Encyclopedia of Homosexuality*. New York: Garland Publishing, Inc.

Elliman, Michael and Roll, Frederick (1986). *The Pink Plaque Guide to London*. London: GMP Publishers.

Fabre, Michel (1991). *From Harlem to Paris: Black American Writers in France, 1840-1980*. Chicago: University of Illinois Press.

Fisher, Helen (1992). *Anatomy of Love*. New York: Fawcett Columbine.

Grief, Martin (1982). *The Gay Book of Days* New York: Carol Publishing Group.

Grier, Barbara and Reid, Coletta (eds.) (1976). *Lesbian Lives: Biographies of Women from* The Ladder. Oakland, CA: Diana Press.

Hadleigh, Boze (1994). *Hollywood Babble On: Stars Gossip About Other Stars*. New York: The Berkeley Publishing Group.

Hadleigh, Boze (1994). *Hollywood Lesbians*. New York: Barricade Books.

Legacies of Love: A Heritage of Queer Bonding
© 2008 by The Haworth Press, Taylor & Francis Group. All rights reserved.
doi:10.1300/5890_10

181

Hirschfeld, Magnus (1910). *Transvestites: The Erotic Drive to Cross-Dress.* New York: Prometheus Books. Translated by Lombardi-Nash, Michael A. (1991).

Katz, Ephraim (1994). *The Film Encyclopedia: Second Edition.* New York: Harper Collins.

Katz, Jonathan (1976). *Gay American History: Lesbians and Gay Men in the USA.* New York: Thomas Y. Crowell Company.

Kayy, W.H. (1965). *The Gay Geniuses.* Glendale, CA: Marvin Miller.

Lauriston, John and Thorstad, David (1974). *The Early Homosexual Rights Movement (1864-1935).* New York: Times Change Press.

Lloyd, Ann and Fuller, Graham (eds.) (1983). *The Illustrated Who's Who of the Cinema.* New York: Macmillan Publishing Co., Inc.

Low, W. Augstus (1981). *Encyclopedia of Black Americans.* New York: McGraw-Hill.

Madsen, Axel (1995). *The Sewing Circle: Hollywood's Greatest Secret Female Stars Who Loved Other Women.* New York: Carol Publishing Group.

Malinowski, Sharon (ed.) (1994). *Gay & Lesbian Literature.* Detroit, MI: St. James Press.

Morin, Jack (1995). *The Erotic Mind.* New York: Harper Collins.

Myron, Nancy & Bunch, Charlotte (eds.) (1974). *Women Remembered.* Baltimore, MD: Diana Press.

Richards, Dell (1990). *Lesbian Lists.* Boston: Alyson Publications, Inc.

Russell, Paul (1995). *The Gay 100: A Ranking of the Most Influential Gay Men and Lesbians, Past and Present.* New York: Citadel Press.

Sicherman, B. and Green, C. H. (eds.) (1980). *Notable American Women.* Cambridge, MA: Belknap Press.

Smith, Jessie Carney (ed.) (1992). *Notable Black American Women.* Detroit, MI: Gale Research, Inc.

Thompson, Mark (ed.) (1994). *Long Road to Freedom: The* Advocate *History of the Gay and Lesbian Movement.* New York: St. Martin's Press.

Tufts, Eleanor (1987). *American Women Artists, 1830-1930.* Washington, DC: The National Museum of Women in the Arts.

Vazzana, Eugene Michael (1995). *Silent Film Necrology.* London: McFarland & Co.

Wallace, Irving, Wallace, Amy, Wallechinsky, David, and Wallace, Sylvia (eds.) (1981). *The Intimate Sex Lives of Famous People.* New York: Delacorte Press.

Image Credits

36　　Raymond Radiguet and Jean Cocteau, June 1922. Public domain.

37　　Oscar Wilde and Lord Alfred Douglas at Oxford, 1894. Public domain.

39　　George Merrill and Edward Carpenter. Courtesy of Director of Culture, Sheffield City Council, Sheffield Archives, Carpenter Collection 8/48, U.K.

41　　Katherine Bradley and Edith Cooper. Public domain.

42　　W. H. Auden. Reproduced by permission of The Huntington Library, San Marino, California, Christopher Isherwood Collection.

43　　Don Bachardy and Christopher Isherwood. Reproduced by permission of The Huntington Library, San Marino, California, The Christopher Isherwood Collection.

44　　Merlo and Williams at St. Mark's Square, Venice, 1948. Reprinted by permission of the Estate of Tennessee Williams, The University of the South.

44　　Merlo and Williams at Key West. Reprinted by permission of the Estate of Tennessee Williams, The University of the South.

45　　Williams and Merlo at South Beach. Reprinted by permission of the Estate of Tennessee Williams, The University of the South.

46　　Sara Teasdale. Public domain.

49　　Ruth Benedict, 1924. Reprinted by permission of The Institute for Intercultural Studies, Inc.

49　　Margaret Mead, 1925. Reprinted by permission of The Institute for Intercultural Studies, Inc.

50　　George Washington Carver, 1906. Johnston, Frances Benjamin, photographer. "George Washington Carver, full-length portrait, standing in field, probably at Tuskegee, holding piece of soil." 1906. Booker T. Washington Collection, Prints and Photograph Division, Library of Congress.

50　　Austin W. Curtis Jr., February 27, 1940. © Bettmann/CORBIS.

51　　Mary Woolley and Jeannette Marks at Fluer de Lys. Mount Holyoke College Library and Special Collections.

52　　Walt Whitman and Peter Doyle, 1865. Public domain.

55　　Malcolm Boyd and Mark Thompson at home in Silverlake, 1988. Photo by Crawford Barton. Reprinted by permission of the San Francisco GLBT Historical Society.

58　　Alexander the Great. Public domain.

60　　Artistic renderings of Sarah Ponsonby and Eleanor Butler. Public domain.

62　　Una Troubridge and Radclyffe Hall with dachshunds. Reprinted by permission of the Harry Ransom Center, The University of Texas at Austin.

63　　S. Josephine Baker. Public domain.

64　　Louise Pearce. Courtesy of the Rockefeller Archive Center.

65　　H.D. and Bryher. Courtesy of the Rosenbach Museum and Library.

66　　Kenneth Macpherson and Bryher at Spitzbergen, 1929. Bryher Papers. General Collection, Beinecke Rare Book and Manuscript Library.

67   ER and Hick on the run. © Bettmann/CORBIS.

68   Eleanor Roosevelt. Public domain.

68   Lorena Hickok. Public domain.

69   FDR with another mistress, Missy Lehand (center), and ER. Public domain.

70   Charlotte Cushman. Public domain.

70   Emma Stebbins. Public domain.

71   Edmonia Lewis. Public domain.

72   Patricia Bresser, Sharon Kowalski, and Karen Thompson. Photo by Les Greene. © Karen Thompson.

76   Queen Christina of Sweden. Public domain.

81   Edward II and Piers Gaveston. Public domain.

85   Amy Lowell, c. 1916. Public domain.

85   Ada Russell, c. 1916. Public domain.

88   Jim Hutton and Freddie Mercury in Munich, 1985. Permission lovingly provided courtesy of Jim Hutton.

90   Lawrence of Arabia, c. 1912. Photo by Ahmed Dahoum. Public domain.

90   Ahmed Dahoum, c. 1912. Photo by Lawrence of Arabia. Public domain.

92   James Baldwin. © Bettmann/CORBIS.

94   Sylvia Beach and Adrienne Monnier at Shakespeare and Co. Sylvia Beach Papers. Manuscripts Division. Department of Rare Books and Special Collections. Princeton University Library.

95   Monnier and Beach. Sylvia Beach Papers. Manuscripts Division. Department of Rare Books and Special Collections. Princeton University Library.

95   Manoly Lascaris and Patrick White on leave together in Beirut. Courtesy of the Estate of Patrick White, National Library of Australia.

96   Karl Giese and Magnus Hirschfeld in exile. Reproduced by permission of The Huntington Library, San Marino, California, The Christopher Isherwood Collection.

102   Eighteenth-century engraving attributed to Anne Bonny. Public domain.

103   Eighteenth-century engraving attributed to Mary Read and Anne Bonny. Public domain.

107   Ted Shawn and Barton Mumaw at Jacob's Pillow, 1932. Courtesy of Jacob's Pillow Dance Festival Archives.

108   Papa Shawn reads the classics to Men Dancers and guest students. Public domain.

109   Will Geer and Raleigh, 1977. Photo by Edmund Teske. © Edmund Teske Archives/Laurence Bump and Nils Vidstrand.

112   Brenda and Wanda Henson at wedding. Photo provided courtesy of Brenda and Wanda Henson.

113 Brenda and Wanda Henson with marriage license in Massachusetts. Photo provided courtesy of Brenda and Wanda Henson.

115 Harmodius and Aristogeiton. National Archaeological Museum, Naples. Photo by Gay Block.

117 Queen Anne. Public domain.

117 Sarah Churchill, Duchess of Marlborough. Public domain.

119 Germaine de Stâel, portrait by Gérard. Public domain.

119 Juliette Récamier, portrait by Gérard. Public domain.

120 Nathalie Micas and Rosa Bonheur. Public domain.

121 Rosa Bonheur and Anna Klumpke. Public domain.

122 William Minnich and Thomas Atwood at Harrisburg, 1864. Public domain.

125 Stephen Foster and George Cooper. Public domain.

126 James Buchanan. Public domain.

126 William Rufus King. Public domain.

127 Abraham Lincoln. Public domain.

127 Joshua Fry Speed. Courtesy of the Abraham Lincoln Presidential Library.

129 Alice Fletcher and Emma Jane Gay cooking out. Public domain.

131 Natalie Barney and Romaine Brooks at Geneva, c. 1915. Public domain.

132 Liane de Pougy and Natalie Barney. Public domain.

132 Natalie Barney and Renée Vivien. Public domain.

133 Natalie Barney and Romaine Brooks. Public domain.

134 Edith Somerville and Violet Martin. Public domain.

135 Willa Cather. Public domain.

135 Edith Lewis, 1902. Public domain.

136 Emma Goldman in Philadelphia mugshot, 1893. Public domain.

137 Mabel Dodge Luhan. Public domain.

139 Angelina Weld Grimké. Public domain.

140 Alberta Hunter. © Getty Images/Frank Driggs Collection.

141 Jackman and Cullen in Paris, 1930s. Courtesy of Michel Fabre, Paris.

142 James Whale. Universal/The Kobal Collection.

143 Mercedes de Acosta and Greta Garbo flee the paparazzi on Hollywood Boulevard, 1931. Courtesy of the Rosenbach Museum and Library.

144 Randolph Scott and Cary Grant at home in the pool. The Kobal Collection.

145 Cary Grant and Randolph Scott sharing a musical moment in their kitchen. Paramount/The Kobal Collection.

146 Marlene Dietrich and Claudette Colbert, June 1935. The Kobal Collection.

147 Danny Kaye performs with Sir Laurence Olivier at the London Palladium, June 22, 1955. AP Images.

148 Jimmie Shields and husband Billy Haines host a party for friend Joan Crawford and her fourth husband Alfred Steele, 1955. Reprinted by permission of William Mann.

150 Margaret Anderson and Jane Heap, early 1920s. Sylvia Beach Papers. Manuscripts Division. Department of Rare Books and Special Collections. Princeton University Library.

152 A smirking J. Edgar Hoover with Clyde Tolson on the boardwalk at Atlantic City, NJ, September 8, 1938. AP Images.

155 Nathan Leopold and Richard Loeb. © Bettmann/CORBIS.

159 Sophia Parnok. Public domain.

159 Marina Tsvetaeva. Public domain.

160 Peter Pears and Benjamin Britten, May 1976. © East Anglian Daily Times. Reprinted by permission of Archant Limited, U.K.

161 Julie and Mary moving to South Africa, 1948. Public domain.

162 Julie and Mary at their home, Delos, on the beach at Camps Bay, Capetown. Public domain.

163 Gertrude Stein and Alice B. Toklas on the terrace at Bilignin, 1938. Photo by Sir Cecil Beaton. © Estate of Cecil Beaton. Reprinted with permission of Sotheby's.

165 Alan Turing getting on the bus. Public domain.

166 Dorothy Thompson in Budapest, age 28. Syracuse University Library. Special Collections Research Center.

166 Christa Winsloe. Syracuse University Library. Special Collections Research Center.

170 Neal Cassady and Jack Kerouac, c. 1952. Reprinted by permission of Carolyn Cassady.

172 Harvey Milk and Joe Campbell, September 1956. Reprinted by permission of the San Francisco History Center, San Francisco Public Library.

174 Paul Monette and Roger Horwitz at the monastery Monte Oliveto, Tuscany, 1983. Photo by Brother John. Courtesy of Winston Wilde.

Cover image credits:

Theatricum Botanicum: Will Geer and Raleigh, © Edmund Teske Archives—Laurence Bump and Nils Vidstrand, reprinted by permission.

Edward Carpenter and George Merrill, from the Carpenter Collection, reprinted courtesy of the Director, Sheffield City Libraries.

Christopher Isherwood and Don Bachardy, from the Christopher Isherwood Collection, Huntington Library, reprinted by permission.

Magnus Hirschfeld and Karl Giese, from the Christopher Isherwood Collection, Huntington Library, reprinted by permission.

Countee Cullen and Harold Jackman, reprinted courtesy of Michel Fabre, Paris.

Benjamin Britten and Peter Pears, reprinted by permission of East Anglian Daily Times/Archant Limited.

Harvey Milk and Joe Campbell, reprinted by permission of the San Francisco Public Library.

All other cover images are in the public domain.

Index

Page numbers followed by the letter "i" indicate illustrations.

Legacies of Love: A Heritage of Queer Bonding
© 2008 by The Haworth Press, Taylor & Francis Group. All rights reserved.
doi:10.1300/5890_11